Good
Morning,
God

WAKE-UP DEVOTIONS TO
START YOUR DAY GOD'S WAY

Good Morning, God
ISBN: 979-8-88898-133-7 - *Paperback*
ISBN: 979-8-88898-134-4 - *Hardcover*
ISBN: 979-8-88898-135-1 - *Ebook*

Copyright © 2024 by Honor Books
Racine, WI

Cover design by Faille Schmitz.
Originally developed by Borden Books.

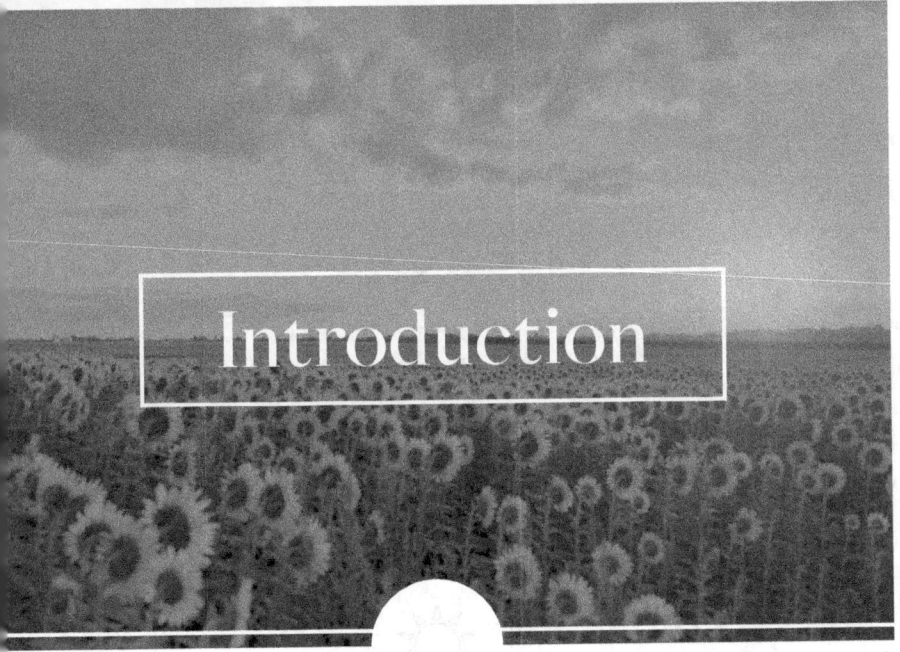

Introduction

All night long, you slept and He watched over you. Before the sun came up. He waited for the moment you would open your eyes and start your day. He loves you. He can't get enough of your company. He has special secrets about the way He designed life—your life—that He wants to let you in on. A few moments each morning with Him can make your whole day wonderful. But how should you start, you ask?

We all know that the way we start our day often shapes our whole approach to the many challenges that cross our paths all day. We know that time with God can really make our day rich and meaningful, not to mention successful in ways we never dreamed were possible. How can we work it in? Mornings are often so full that we feel lucky to get out the door with our shoes matching. How in the world can we make time to think about the kinds of things that change our lives and brighten our days?

Good Morning, God is a collection of short meditations and stories to make it possible to fit a quiet, life-changing moment into your morning.

Read the short entry and the Bible verse. Think about the nudges you feel in your heart—you know, the ones you feel when God speaks to you. Talk to Him about those. It won't take long, and that precious time can transform your day.

The First Morning

What a joy it must have been for the first man and woman to awaken that first morning after their creation!

Before them lay a beautiful garden without blemish, a harmonious creation without turmoil, an orderly environment without a weed or thorn. Most wonderful of all, they freely walked and talked with the Lord in the cool of the day. Wouldn't you love to experience that glorious state for one morning! Eleanor Farjeon must have felt the same elation when she penned the words to her now internationally famous hymn:

> *"Morning has broken like the first morning;*
> *Blackbird has spoken like the first bird.*
> *Praise for the singing! Praise for the Morning!*
> *Praise for them, springing fresh from the Word!*
>
> *Sweet the rain's new fall sunlit from heaven,*
> *Like the first dew-fall on the first grass.*
> *Praise for the sweetness of the wet garden,*
> *Spring in completeness where his feet pass.*
> *Mine is the sunlight! Mine is the morning*
> *Born of the one light Eden saw play!*
> *Praise with elation, praise every morning,*
> *God's recreation of the new day!"[1]*

While we may not awaken to a perfect, pristine world in our natural bodies, we can awaken to a "brand-new day" in our minds and hearts. We can walk and talk with the Lord all day long. Each day the Lord presents to His beloved children wondrous possibilities to explore with Him.

Let us always remember that He is the Creator and our loving Father. No matter what state we find ourselves in. He can create something new in us, for us, and through us. What cause for praise! His next act of creation is waiting to unfold as we yield our life to Him this morning and throughout our day!

His compassions fail not.
They are new every morning.

LAMENTATIONS
3:22-23 NKJV

Turn On the Headlights

A woman confessed to a friend her confusion and hesitancy about an important life decision she faced. She professed to believe in God, but could not bring herself to rely on her faith to make that decision that weighed heavily on her.

"How can I know I'm doing the right thing?" she asked. "How can I possibly believe my decision will be right when I can't even see tomorrow?"

Her friend thought and then replied, "Here's how I look at it. When you drive down a dark country road without streetlights to offer you any notion of where you are, it's a little scary. You must rely on your headlights. They may only show you ten yards of the road in front of you, but you can see where to go for that little stretch of the road. As you travel the distance, the headlights show you ten more yards, and then ten more, until eventually you reach your destination safely."

When you come to the edge of all the light you know
and are about to step off into the darkness of the unknown,
faith is knowing one of two things will happen:
There will be something solid to stand on,
or you will be taught how to fly.[2]

Thy word is a lamp unto my feet, and a light unto my path.

PSALM 119:105 KJV

You are Precious

A young woman named June volunteered at a church agency that served the poor and homeless of her city. One day June met George, who had come in to receive some help. Winter was coming and he needed a jacket and some shoes to help keep him warm.

He took a seat in the chapel because the waiting room was crowded and noisy. When he indicated he wanted a Bible, June went to get one for him while he waited his turn in the clothing room. When she returned with a Bible, she sat down to talk to him for a while.

George looked like he was in his late 50s or early 60s. June noticed his thin hair beginning to gray and the deep lines which marked his face. His hands were stiff and he had lost part of one finger. Although it was 1:30 in the afternoon, he smelled slightly of alcohol. He was a short, slight man, and he spoke softly. He had come into the agency alone, and June wondered if he had any family—anyone who cared that he existed.

June wrote George's name in the front of his Bible along with the date. Then she showed him the study helps in the back, which would help him find key passages.

As they talked, the thought occurred to June: George is one of God's very precious creatures. She wondered if George knew that. She wondered how long it had been since someone had told him. What if no one had ever told him he was precious to God— and to all God's other children as well?

George had very little influence or stature, but God spoke to June through him that day, "My children need to know they are precious to Me. Please tell them that." Since then, she has made that message a part of every encounter she has at the church agency.

Ask the Lord how you might share the message, "You are precious to God," with others today through your words and actions.

Since thou wast precious in my sight, thou hast been honourable, and I have loved thee.

ISAIAH 43:4 KJV

The Bigger Picture

D uring World War II, thousands in factories across the United States constructed parachutes. From the worker's point of view, the job was tedious. It required stitching endless lengths of colorless fabric, crouched over a sewing machine eight to ten hours a day. A day's work produced a formless, massive heap of cloth with no visible resemblance to a parachute.

In order to motivate workers and keep them concerned with quality, the management in one factory held a meeting. Management informed workers each day of the approximate number of parachutes that had been strapped to the back of pilots, copilots, and other "flying" personnel the previous day. They learned just how many men had jumped to safety from disabled planes as a result of their high-quality work. The managers encouraged their workers to see the big picture on their job.

As a second means of motivation, the workers were asked to form a mental picture of a husband, brother, or son who might be the one saved by the parachute they sewed.

That factory held one of the highest levels of quality on record![3]

Don't let the tedium of each day's chores and responsibilities wear you down so you only see the "stitching" in front of you. Keep your eyes on the big picture. Focus on why you do what you do and who will benefit from your work, including those you don't know and may never meet. You may not have all the answers to the question, "Why am I here?" but you can rest assured, the Lord does!

Ultimately, the Bible tells us we will be in heaven for eternity—and that is the biggest picture of all! God is preparing us for heaven, just as fie is preparing heaven for us. He is creating us to be the people He wants to live with forever.

Whatever mundane tasks or trivial pursuits you undertake today, see them in the light of eternity. They will take on a whole new meaning!

"I go to prepare a place for you. And if I go and prepare a place for you. I will come again and receive you to myself; that where I am, there you may be also."

JOHN 14:2-3 NKJV

A Familiar Voice

A young mother alone with her preschoolers for a week while her husband was away on a business trip found the fourth day particularly exasperating. After several bedtime stories, she finally succeeded in putting the energetic children to bed and decided to relax. She changed into an old pair of sweats and began to shampoo her hair when she heard the children jumping around in their room.

Wrapping a towel around her head, she went to scold them. As she walked out of the children's room, she overhead the littlest one ask, "Who was that?"

In our busy lives we often overlook God's presence. We can become so involved in the task at hand that we fail to recognize His voice Then we miss His guidance and grace. Have you ever found yourself asking, "Who was that?" only later to realize that is was indeed God?

He wants us to know Him so well that we immediately recognize His voice and obey His commands. There is no better way to know His voice than through an intimate relationship with Him.

A perfect time to develop an awareness of the Father's voice is in the early morning when we can quietly listen.

"The sheep follow him because they know his voice."

JOHN 10:4 NASB

Only Imagine

I n his classic self-help book *Think and Grow Rich*, Napoleon Hill wrote, "Whatever the mind of man can conceive and believe, he can achieve." His premise, and that of many others, is that once the human mind is programmed with a certain expectation, it will begin to fulfill that expectation.

The Scriptures declared this principle long before Hill wrote his book. Faith believes and then sees. It is the expectation of a miracle before it occurs.

The Aluminum Company of America coined an interesting word: imagineering. They combined the idea of imagining a product or service, with the idea that the dream would then be engineered into a reality. Throughout history we've seen this principle at work.

> • *A primitive ancestor came up with the idea that it was easier to roll objects than drag them—and he carved a wheel from stone.*
> • *A man named Gutenberg imagined that letters might be set in metal and combined to create words, which then could be printed repeatedly with the application of ink. He set about to make such a machine.*
> • *Men designed cathedrals that took decades to build—but build them they did.*

Ideas and dreams you have today will directly influence your future. What you begin to believe for, and then how you act on that belief, will result in what you have, do, and are in the days, weeks, months, and years ahead.

Let your "faith imagination" soar today. Believe for God's highest and best in your life. Then begin to live and work as if that miracle is on its way.

Faith is the substance of things hoped for, the evidence of things not seen.

HEBREWS 11:1 NKJV

Share Your Morning

Most people wake up to an alarm clock ringing at an appointed hour rather than to a rooster crowing in the barnyard. However, for the apostle Peter the crowing rooster on the early morning of Jesus' crucifixion was a wake-up call. It woke him up to who he really was. In Peter's worst moment, he denied his friend and teacher, Jesus. He wept bitterly over his betrayal, and must have experienced terrible guilt and shame.

One morning after His resurrection, Jesus appeared to the disciples, who were fishing at the Sea of Tiberias. He called out from the shore and asked if they had caught any fish. The disciples didn't recognize Him and called back, "No." Jesus told them to throw the net on the other side of the boat, and the catch was so great they were unable to haul it in. They then knew the man directing them was Jesus and headed to shore.

When the disciples arrived, Jesus invited them to eat with Him. "Come and have breakfast," He said. In the dawning hours of the day, the resurrected Jesus cooked breakfast for them.

How do you think Peter felt when, after the greatest failure of his life, Jesus wanted to spend time with him, eat with him, and even help him fish? Jesus sought out the disciple who had let Him down when He needed him most. Moreover, He called Peter to lead His followers.

Like Peter, there are experiences in our days that serve

as "wake-up calls" to who we claim to be. Those "wake-up calls" come in the form of opportunities to compromise who we are and what we believe. How do we act when others aren't around? How do we handle situations that can violate our integrity? To live a compromised life is to deny Jesus—just as Peter did. (See Titus 1:16.)

It is always important for us to spend time with the Lord, but when we need to come clean in our heart, it is especially important. Jesus always invites us to fellowship with Him. He always forgives.

Whatever mistakes or compromises we made yesterday, Jesus still loves us today and says, "Come and share your morning with Me."

"You, O Lord . . . know the hearts
of all."

ACTS 1:24 NKJV

Look with the Heart

Maria, a kindhearted teacher's aide, simply wanted to "love the children better" in the class for emotionally disturbed students. She could tolerate much, but Danny wore her patience out. It proved easier to love him when he tried to hurt himself rather than others. Although Danny was only seven years old, it really hurt when he hit Maria.

For months Danny withdrew into a private world and tried to hit his head against a wall any time he became upset. But now, he was making progress because his actions changed from withdrawal to striking out at Maria.

"Progress?" exclaimed Maria. "How is it progress for him to want to hurt me?"

"Danny was repeatedly abused as a small child," explained the school psychologist. "He has known only adults who were mean to him or simply ignored his most basic needs. He has had no one he could trust. No one to hold him close; no one to dry his tears when he cried or fix him food when he was hungry. He experienced punishment without reason. He's making progress because for the first time in his life, he trusts an adult enough to act out his anger rather than self-destruct. You are that trustworthy adult, Maria."

Tears spilled from Maria's eyes upon hearing the explanation as she exclaimed, "I see!" As comprehension dawned, her anger quickly melted.

John Ruskin wrote, "When love and skill work together, expect a masterpiece."[4]

Sometimes progress seems elusive, but God faithfully continues the good work He started in each of our lives. If we will open the eyes of our hearts, we will see His hand at work in our midst.

"Give your servant a discerning heart."

1 KINGS 3:9

Friends

The predawn air had a distinct chill to it when the pickup truck horn sounded each morning that summer. Rob would wander out to the truck where Ben waited. Farmers hired Ben with his New Holland hay stacker to collect the baled hay from their fields and build large square haystacks for feeding the livestock during the winter.

The work itself was always the same, but the ease of doing it varied tremendously because of the type of hay. Alfalfa made tight, hard bales that were easy to handle. Wheat made looser bales that were apt to break apart and thus were much more work.

The first thing, Rob would ask, "Are we working wheat again today?" He always hoped for alfalfa, but without fail, it seemed, Ben would respond, "Yep, wheat it is." Rob would then doze until they arrived at the fields. Once there, they enjoyed a cup of coffee and watched the sun rise into the still morning air before the long day of hard work. Neither said much during those times, nor was it necessary.

Ben retired and Rob has a family of his own. They rarely see one another now, but when they do, it doesn't take long for the conversation to turn to that special summer. Each man recalls different lessons learned from their work together, but a common one is their shared belief that finding God's will requires a commitment to serving Him no matter how hard—or easy—the work.

God's presence is like that. It's not what is said or not said that matters so much as it is the being together and the lessons we learn.

It is you, a man like myself, my companion, my close friend.

PSALM 55:13

Rush Hour

So many of us find the morning as a rush hour. Various family members scurry in different directions with various needs and diverse timetables. One has lost a sock; another can't find last night's homework. One needs a sack lunch; another needs lunch money. One leaves with a kiss, another with a shout, and another needs encouragement to open her eyes as she stumbles out the door.

A "quiet time" in the morning to center ourselves and to renew our relationship with our Heavenly Father stands in sharp contrast. Carving out that time for yourself may be your supreme challenge of the day, but it is an effort worth its weight in gold, as so aptly stated by Bruce Fogarty:

THE MORNING HOUR

Alone with God, in quiet peace.
From earthly cares, I find release;
New strength I borrow for each day
As there with God, I stop to pray.

Alone with God, my sins confess'd,
He speaks in mercy, I am blest.
I know the kiss of pardon free,
I talk to God, He talks to me.

26

Alone with God, my vision clears,
I see my guilt, the wasted years.
I plead for grace to walk His way
And live for Him, from day to day.

Alone with God no sin between,
His lovely face so plainly seen;
Mj guilt all gone, my heart at rest
With Christ, my Lord, my soul is blest.

Lord, keep my life alone for Thee;
From sin and self, Lord, set me free.
And when no more this earth I trod,
They'll say, "He walked alone with God."[5]

Be still, and know that I am God; I
will be exalted among the nations,
I will be exalted in the earth!

PSALM 46:10 NKJV

Forever There

A businessman once said: "Sometimes, after waking in the morning, I am appalled by the thought of all the duties and appointments that await me in the next eight or ten hours."

"Then I repeat to myself the words: 'in quietness and confidence shall be thy strength'; and Thou wilt keep him in perfect peace, whose mind is stayed on thee.' It is astonishing how quickly the load is lifted once I remind myself of God's presence and help. The strain and tension disappear and in its place a feeling of serenity and peace wells up within me."

Dr. Frank Laubach learned to be aware of the presence of God by disciplining his thoughts to think on God once every minute. He called it "the game of the minutes." Jacob Boehm, a sixteenth-century saint, also spoke of a practice that involved an almost continual awareness of God's presence: "If Thou dost once every hour throw thyself . . . into the abysmal mercy of God, then thou shalt receive power to rule over death and sin."

The airplane pilot radios a message to a control tower every hour and receives an answer. Thus he keeps "on the beam." He is in touch with the controller; he receives his orders, and reports his position. He knows if the station does not hear from him at the appointed time, they will be alerted to the fact he and his passengers may be in danger.

Not everyone has Laubach's or Boehm's discipline.

Wouldn't it be reassuring to talk to and hear from the control tower at least every hour during the day? It is as simple as uttering a prayer or repeating a Scripture—"Thou wilt keep me in perfect peace."

Thou wilt keep him in perfect peace, whose mind is stayed on thee; because he trusteth in thee.

ISAIAH 26:3 KJV

Make It Right

Bruce Catton, a great Civil War historian, wrote numerous well-known books, including *A Stillness at Appomattox*. In the opinion of former Congressman and U. S. ambassador Fred J. Eckert, Catton had a wonderful way of dealing with his errors.

Eckert read one of Catton's books, *This Hallowed Ground*, as a high-school sophomore. Moved by it, he sought out other books on the Civil War. He discovered Catton had made a mistake in *This Hallowed Ground*. He had transposed the names of a first and second officer.

Eckert's teacher encouraged him to write Catton about the mistake. When he did, Catton responded by sending him autographed copies of several of his books, including a copy of *This Hallowed Ground*. In it he wrote, "To Fred Eckert, who caught me napping at Fort Donelson."

Eckert says he learned a valuable lesson from this experience: If you always do your best, you probably won't make too many serious errors. And when you do slip up from time to time, the best thing to do is acknowledge it and move on.[6]

Many of us spend a great deal of time and effort to justify or cover our sins and mistakes. The truth is, it is much easier to confess those sins, ask God's forgiveness, seek the forgiveness of others involved, and then move forward.

Human pride hinders us from acknowledging our

mistakes. Perhaps that is the reason pride is often considered the chief of all sins. It keeps us from repentance, which cuts off our intimacy with God.

Start your day with a clean slate. Ask the Lord to forgive you of anything left unforgiven. Accept His forgiveness. Make amends as necessary. Then press forward to live the life the Lord has called you to!

If we confess our sins, he is faithful and just and will forgive us our sins and purify us from all unrighteousness.

1 JOHN 1:9

Consider Change

A lecturer once told a story of a counseling patient who hated her job and thought it was ruining her life. However throughout her therapy, she seemed completely unwilling to improve her situation.

When he suggested she hunt for a new job, she complained that there were no decent jobs in her small town. He asked if she had considered looking for a job in the next town, fifteen miles away. She told him she would need a car to travel that far, and she didn't have one.

When the therapist offered a plan to purchase an inexpensive car, she countered that it would never work, because there was no place to park in the neighboring town anyway!

Many have said that three things in life are certain: death, taxes, and change. If you look around, you'll notice that most people can deal with the first two better than change. But without it, we'll never know how wonderful the plans God has for us can be.

Fear of change comes from fear of loss, even if it might be the loss of something we never liked in the first place. If you struggle with change in your life today, take a moment to bring your fears to the Lord. With faith in His guidance, change can lead to a blessing!

> Our real blessings often appear to us
> In the shapes of pains, losses, and disappointments;
> But let us have patience,
> And we soon shall see them in their proper figures.[7]

God has not given us a
spirit of fear,
but of power
and of love
and of a sound mind.

2 TIMOTHY 1:7 NKJV

Land of the Midnight Sun

In Barrow, Alaska, morning takes on a completely new meaning. At 330 miles from the Arctic Circle and almost as close to the North Pole, Barrow is the real-life "Land of the Midnight Sun." For 83 days, from May 11 to August 1, the sun never sinks below the horizon.

The dark side to life exists at high latitudes. Each year on November 18, residents watch the last sunset of the year as the sun dips below the horizon and will not return for more than two months.

While not pitch-black all the time, winter in Barrow is truly a season of darkness. Temperatures dip so low that fuel oil congeals. Keys snap like toothpicks in frozen locks. Windchills near 100 below can cause frostbite in 30 seconds.

The perpetual dark, cold, and wind can seem oppressive to those who take the daily blush of the sun for granted. Residents admit that dreams of Hawaii are common.

Not everyone wants to leave, though. "Many people here truly like the winter, enjoying the peace and quiet," says Barrow Mayor Jim Vorderstrasse. "A lot of it reflects on a person's outlook on life. You can sit around being depressed, or you can get up and find something worthwhile to do."[8]

Seasons of darkness can occur in anyone's life. Often our outlook determines how we handle those difficult times. We can shut ourselves in and yearn for another life, or we can rely on God's Light to help us find a life of hope and serenity. The choice is always ours.

Not that I speak in respect of want: for I have learned, in whatsoever state I am, therewith to be content.

PHILIPPIANS 4:11-12 KJV

Eternal Purpose

As a child, did you ever try to reroute a small stream by building a dam across the water with rocks and stones? Did you ever build a mud dam to collect the flowing water and make a pool in which to sail your toy boat? Our childlike efforts were never completely successful, were they? The stones eventually gave way to the rush of water and the mud dam finally washed downstream.

For 5,000 years, dams have been utilized to control water—to prevent floods, divert rivers, store water, and irrigate land. Even today's modern dams do not completely stop the flow of water back into the streams or prevent its eventual return to the oceans.

Every day we meet challenges that can potentially divert us and even temporarily defeat God's purpose for our life. Failures, bad decisions, or mistakes may have derailed our lives, but if we give those circumstances to the Lord, they will never defeat His plan for us. In fact, we are usually in awe as He takes those circumstances and uses them to accomplish His good and eternal purpose. (See Romans 8:28.)

God's plan can never be defeated—and that is good news for you today. God is in control, which means nothing that happens can cause Him defeat, even the willful disobedience of one person, or a group of people.

If that is true for the Sovereign of the Universe, it is

also true for us if we align our purposes with His. Although God's will for our lives may be temporarily diverted by our sins or mistakes, by circumstances, or even by the harm someone else inflicts on us, we can never be ultimately defeated as long as we cooperate with Him.[9]

What shall we then say to these things? If God be for us, who can be against us?

ROMANS 8:31 KJV

Never-Ending Supply

I t is easier to thank the Lord after we have seen His work. We have something to go back to and rejoice over. It is not as easy to be thankful for what we don't see or haven't experienced.

A mother purchased a new violin for her son. Together they had saved for months to afford this fine instrument. He promised to care for it, but it wasn't long before the boy forgot his promise and left his violin on the porch overnight. The cold night air and the heavy morning dew caused the violin to bulge. The sound quality was no longer the same.

The boy's mother took this opportunity to teach her son a lesson for life. She decided to show her son what went into the creation of the violin.

She took him to the store where they purchased the violin. They visited a violin manufacturing company and went to a lumber mill where the wood had been carefully chosen for such a fine instrument. They even visited a forest where trees grew specifically for quality instruments. The mother and son also made trips to learn how the bow and strings were manufactured. She wanted her son to understand why he should be thankful for the beautiful musical instrument with which he had been blessed.

God wants our thanks, and He has provided us with a never-ending supply of reminders of why we should be grateful to Him. When you begin your day in an attitude of gratefulness, it leaves little room for complaints and much room for grace to flourish.

I will give thanks to the
Lord with all my heart.

PSALM 9:1 NASB

Now Moments

Morning is a great time to make a list of "things to do" and plan the day. It's also the best time to tackle those tasks that are the most difficult or we like least. If we procrastinate as the day wears on, rationalization sets in and sometimes even the tasks we had considered most important remain undone.

Here's a little poem just for those who struggle with procrastination:

HOW AND WHEN

We are often greatly bothered
By two fussy little men,
Who sometimes block our pathway
Their names are How and When.

If we have a task or duty
Which we can put off a while,
And we do not go and do it
You should see those two rogues smile!

But there is a way to beat them,
And I will tell you how:
If you have a task or duty,
Do it well, and do it now.

Unknown

As part of your morning prayer time, ask the Lord to help you to overcome any tendency to procrastinate and prioritize projects according to His plans and purposes.

Often we ask the Lord, "What do You want me to do?" but then fail to ask Him one of the key follow-up questions, "When do You want me to do this?" When we have a sense of God's timing, and in some cases His urgency about a matter, our conviction grows to accomplish the job right away.

God's "omnipresence" means He is always with you, and He is always "timely." He's with you in the "now" moments of your life. He is concerned with how you use every moment of your time. Recognize that He desires to be part of your time-management and task-completion process today!

I will hasten and not delay to obey
your commands.

PSALM 119:60

Strangers

Sheila paused at the door of the small country church, uncertain. *It's so quiet in here, she thought. I will just sit and rest for a moment, and then I will be on my way.* She didn't mean to fall asleep. It was just so warm and comfortable and she was so tired.

As she settled into the back pew, the air included the slight mustiness of worn rugs mixed with the smell of furniture polish, and dust mites danced in the sunbeams coming through the broad windows. As her eyelids grew heavy, she could hear the building settle with minute creaks and groans. Somewhere in the sunshine outside, she heard the sparkling laughter of a young child at play. Then her eyes closed and she slept.

The young pastor came from his study near the front of the church and headed to the parsonage. He was surprised to see Sheila on the back pew, head resting against the high-end piece, sound asleep.

Why, she couldn't be more than fourteen or fifteen. She must have run away from home, he thought.

Slipping out quietly, he went next door to the parsonage and asked his wife Brenda to come back to the church with him. Brenda gently awakened Sheila. Although she was embarrassed to be found asleep in the church. Sheila quickly responded to Brenda's gentle love and concern. The church offered food, shelter, clothing, and prayerful compassion to Sheila. In the years to come, she often thought of that small

42

church and the caring couple she met there.

It was a memory she savored. As she moved from shelter to shelter, she would often tell anyone who would listen that on one occasion, she met Jesus, and His name was Brenda.

Be not forgetful to entertain strangers.

HEBREWS 13:2 KJV

Co-Creators with Him!

Serendipity, according to *Merriam-Webster's Collegiate Dictionary*, is "the faculty or phenomenon of finding valuable or agreeable things not sought for."[10] We sometimes call it an "accident, dumb luck, or fate," but serendipity has given us new products and better ways of doing things.

Examples of serendipity include Columbus's discovery of America while searching for a route to India. Native Americans discovered maple syrup when, in need of water, they tapped a maple tree and made the first maple syrup as they boiled off the sap. Westward-traveling pioneers looking for water stopped at a stream for a drink and found gold nuggets in the water.

While George Balias drove his car through a car wash, he lived a moment of serendipity that made him a millionaire. As he watched the strings of the brushes cleaning his car, he turned his mind to his list of things to do, among them edging his lawn.

Suddenly an idea "popped" into his head. He took another long look at the strings on the rotating brush. The strings straightened out when turning at high speed, but were still flexible enough to reach into every nook and cranny of his car to get it clean. He asked himself, *Why not use a nylon cord, whirling at high speed, to trim the grass and weeds around the trees and the house?* His idea—his serendipity—led to the invention of the Weedeater.

Where do we get new ideas? God is the Master behind serendipity! He may not always give you a million-dollar idea, but He can cause you to be more creative. One expert gives this advice: Capture the ideas, jot them down quickly before they are gone, and evaluate later. Take time to daydream with the Lord. Seek new challenges. Expand your perspective. Learn and do new things.[11]

Remember today that God is your Creator and the Creator of everything in the universe. Ask Him to inspire you with new ideas that can glorify Him and benefit others. We are co-creators with Him!

We are his workmanship, created
in Christ Jesus unto good works.

EPHESIANS 2:10 KJV

If You Believe You Can, You Can

You can do anything. That's what Kent Cullers' parents told him as he grew up. That's what many parents tell their children. However, Cullers was born blind. Even so, if a child hears the phrase, "You can do anything" often enough, it sinks in. It bears fruit. It certainly did in Cullers' case.

As a young boy he insisted on climbing trees and riding a bicycle. His father arranged a job transfer to California so the boy could attend a regular school, and Cullers became a straight-A student. He graduated valedictorian of his high-school class and a National Merit Scholar. He went on to earn a Ph.D. in physics.

Cullers' first love was forever space, so it seems fitting that he found himself employed at NASA. As a researcher, one of his jobs was to design equipment to help scientists search for signs of intelligent communication in outer space.[12]

How does a blind man see what others can't? He uses his "mind's eye." He also uses his other senses— perhaps a little better than most people. Above all, he continues to tell himself what his parents taught him early in life: You can do anything.

The apostle Paul would have added a key phrase to Cullers' advice from his parents: through Christ who gives me strength. The source of all our ability, energy, and creativity is the Lord Himself. It is He who challenges us to go forward and equips us to get the task done. It is the Lord working in us to enable us, working through us to empower us, and working on our behalf to enrich us.

At the same time, the Lord expects us to do two things: first, to open ourselves to His presence and power; and second, to get in gear. He calls us to believe and do.

What do you believe today? What are you doing? Activate both your believing and doing, synchronize both with the will of God, and you can't help but be launched to a higher and better position.

I can do all things through Christ
who strengthens me.

PHILIPPIANS 4:13
NKJV

If Only for One

Some days it's hard just to get out of bed. Our motivation fades or is completely gone. We are overcome with a "What difference does it make?" attitude. We become overwhelmed at the enormity of the duties before us. Our talents and resources seem minuscule in comparison to the task.

A businessman and his wife once took a much-needed getaway at an oceanside hotel. During their stay, a powerful storm arose, lashing the beach and sending massive breakers against the shore. The storm woke the man. He lay still in bed listening to the storm's fury and reflected on his own life of constant and continual demands and pressures.

Before daybreak the wind subsided. The man climbed out of bed and went outside to survey the damage done by the storm. As he walked along the beach, he noticed the starfish that covered the sand thrown ashore by the massive waves. Unable to get to the water, the starfish faced inevitable death as the sun's rays dried them out.

Down the beach, the man saw a figure walking along the shore. The figure would stoop and pick something up. In the dim of the early-morning twilight, he couldn't quite make it out. As he approached, he realized a young boy was picking up the starfish one at a time and flinging them back into the ocean to safety.

As the man neared the young boy he said, "Why are you doing that? One person will never make a difference—

there are too many starfish to get back into the water before the sun comes up."

The boy said sadly, "Yes, that's true," as he bent to pick up another starfish. Then he said, "But I can sure make a difference to that one."

God never intended for an individual to solve all of life's problems. He intended for each one of us to use whatever resources and gifts He gave us to make a difference where we are.[13]

"There is joy in the presence of
the angels of God over one sinner
who repents."

LUKE 15:10 NASB

Equality

I magine you are a twenty-one-year-old young man, father of a baby son, and divorced. You have been raised in church your entire life where divorce is a failure to be prayed for but avoided. As a divorce you are termed unclean. With that mind-set, Horace scheduled an appointment to speak with his pastor.

Pastor Hale met Horace at the door of his office with a warm smile and firm handshake. Much to Horace's surprise, he did not direct him to the chair in front of his desk and return to his high-backed leather seat behind it. Instead, the pastor took his seat in a comfortable chair and motioned Horace to sit on the adjacent couch. This simple gesture of sitting without a desk between them overwhelmed Horace.

To Horace's way of thinking, the pastor was holy and he was unfit. Yet, the pastor treated him as though his needs were the only thing that interested him. His actions said, "I do not consider myself better than you simply because God has called me to serve as pastor for this church. I am here to serve you, and I want you to feel comfortable because you are important to me just as you are today."

Horace's torment and doubt began to ease. A sense of rest and assurance comforted his hurting heart.

Although divorce is commonplace in today's world, this does nothing to minimize its pain for those experiencing it. If you have the chance, be a Pastor Hale to a Horace today—your life and theirs will be all the richer for your caring.

Be at rest once more,
O my soul.

PSALM 116:7

A Reflection of Forgiveness

It's hard to start the day when you continue to carry a hurt you have not forgiven. One morning, Denise Stovall's daughter Deanna taught her a special lesson about forgiveness.

"Mama! How do you spell 'Louis'?" Deanna asked as she rushed into the kitchen.

"Louis? Who's Louis?" asked Denise.

"You know," said the five-year-old. "He's the boy who gave me my black eye."

For several days Denise had asked herself how one child could be so mean to another child. Anger sizzled inside her every time she saw the black and blue mark around Deanna's bright, hazel eye. Slamming the oven door closed as if it were the person in question, she said, "Why on earth do you want to know how to spell his name—especially after what he did to you?"

Deanna's reply reminded Denise of why Jesus said, "Let the little children come unto me, for of such is the kingdom of Heaven."

"W-e-l-l, at church yesterday, Miss Mae told us we should make paper chains for All Saints Day. She said to make a ring every time somebody does a nice thing like Jesus did, and then put that person's name on the ring. Louis told me on the bus today that he was sorry he hit me in my eye, and that was nice. I want to put his name on this ring and make it part of the chain, so we can pray for him so he won't do it again."

As Denise stood in the middle of the kitchen with her hands on her hips, the words of a recent sermon came back to convict her: "Forgiveness, no matter how long it takes or how difficult it is to attain, is the only path to healing and freedom."

Upon reflection, Denise thought Deanna's bruised eyelid looked just a little better.[14]

Before you start the day, make certain you are free from all unforgiveness and offense. Remember how much God has forgiven you, and it will be easier to forgive others!

"Forgive us our debts, as we also have forgiven our debtors."

MATTHEW 6:12

Reciprocity

Sometimes when we focus on helping others, we solve our own problems. That certainly proved true for David, an eight-year-old from Wisconsin with a speech impediment. His problem made him hesitant to read aloud or speak up in class.

David's mother also had a problem—multiple sclerosis. One winter day while she and David walked, her cane slipped on an icy patch and caused her to fall. She was unhurt, but the incident left David with the desire to do something to help her.

Some time later, David's teacher assigned her class to create an invention for a national contest. He decided he would invent a cane that wouldn't slide on ice by putting a nail on the bottom of it. After his mother expressed concern about the nail damaging floor coverings, he developed a retractable system. Much like a ballpoint pen, the nail popped out of sight when a button at the top of the cane was released.

David's invention earned him first prize in the contest. As the winner, he was required to make public appearances and communicate with those who expressed an interest in his project. The more he talked about the cane, the less noticeable his speech impediment became![15]

Who needs your help today?

They may not need you to invent something for them. They may simply need your assistance on a project, a word of encouragement, or prayer for a particular need. As you extend the effort, time, and energy to help someone, you will find something inside you healed, renewed, or strengthened. An outward expression toward others always does something inwardly that enables, empowers, and enhances the character of Christ Jesus in us.

That's God's principle of reciprocity!

Pray for each other so that you
may be healed.

JAMES 5:16

Our Finest Hour

Sir Winston Churchill, the irascible leader of Britain during World War II, is one of the most well-known world leaders of modern times. People often forget he is also associated with one of the most ignoble defeats in modern British history—the disastrous Gallipoli campaign of World War I that forced his resignation from the admiralty in 1915 and nearly destroyed his career.[16]

Quit? Not Winston Churchill! In fact, twenty-five years later on May 10, 1940, he succeeded Neville Chamberlain as prime minister. However, the days that followed are considered among the darkest of all British history.

World War II brought with it Dunkerque and the fall of France. London found itself bombed nightly during the infamous blitz. It was precisely during these times that Churchill urged his compatriots to conduct themselves so that, "if the British Empire and its Commonwealth last for a thousand years, men will still say, 'This was their finest hour.'"[17]

Did Churchill ever have doubts about the outcome of the world conflict that threatened to destroy all that he loved? It would be only human. Regardless, he lived his challenge to his countrymen. He did indeed conduct himself so historians consider that time to be "his finest hour." In simple terms, "He walked the walk and talked the talk."

In that sense, Churchill and other world leaders we

admire are not so different from each of us. We, too, are challenged to live every day with integrity and consistency. We are just as capable to live our lives in such a manner that when we face our challenges it can be said of us, it was our finest hour.

The just man walketh in his integrity.

PROVERBS 20:7 KJV

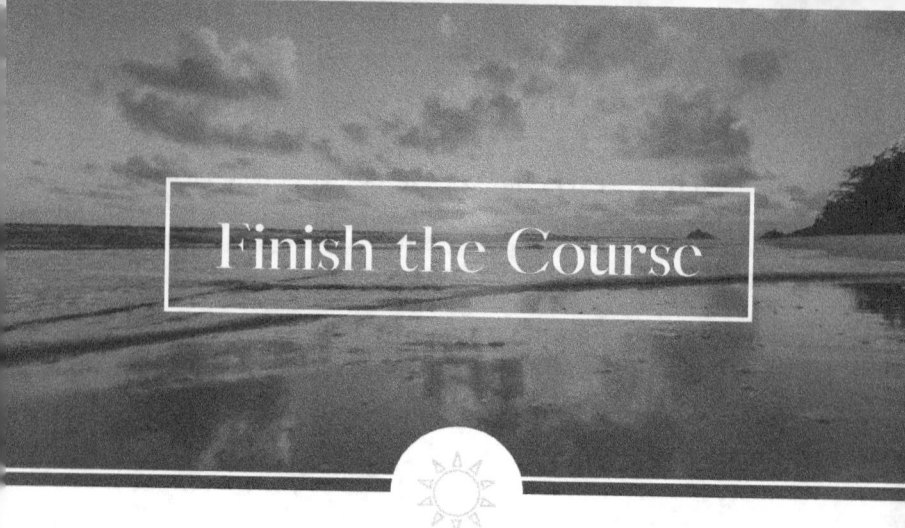

Finish the Course

The Saturday of the dog sled derby dawned as a bright, clear, cold winter morning. The people of the small Wisconsin town on the southern shore of Lake Superior looked forward to the annual competition. Little fir trees set into the surface of the frozen lake marked out the one-mile course across the ice. Spectators standing on the steep slope along the shore had a good view of the entire course.

The contestants were all children ranging from large, older boys with several dogs and big sleds to one little guy who appeared to be no more than five years old. He entered the race with a little sled pulled by his small dog and lined up with the rest of the entrants waiting for the race to begin.

When the signal sounded to declare the start of the race, the racers took off in a flurry that quickly outdistanced the youngest contestant and his little dog. In fact, the larger and more experienced racers disappeared so quickly down the course that the little guy seemed hardly in the race at all. The contest was going well, however, and although in last place, the little fellow stayed in the competition, enjoying every minute.

About halfway around the course, the dog team in second place began to overtake the lead team. The dogs came too close to the lead team and soon the two dog teams began to fight. As each sled reached the fighting, snarling animals, they joined in the fracas.

None of the drivers successfully steered their teams clear of the growling brawl. Soon all of the dogs and racers became one big seething mass of kids, sleds, and dogs—all that is, but the little fellow and his one dog. He managed to stay the course and was the only one to finish the race.[18]

Each day holds the potential for something to sidetrack us from our intended purpose. No matter how great the distraction, we can finish the course if we stay on target!

He [Jesus] steadfastly set his face
to go to Jerusalem.

LUKE 9:51 KJV

Waves

Early in the morning a lake is usually very still; no animals, no people, no noise, no boats, or cars. All is quiet.

This is the best time to skip rocks. By taking a small flat pebble and throwing it at the right angle, you can skip it across the water leaving circles of ripples every time it makes contact with the water.

The ripples form small and much defined circles at first, then they spread out and break apart until they vanish. If several people skip rocks at the same time, the ripples cross over one another and blend together to make mini-waves across the lake. It can be an amazing impact.

For most of us, mornings quickly fill with many needs that require our attention and we find it difficult to spend time alone with God. However, the Lord set a marvelous example for us by rising early to listen to God. If we make no time for this quiet morning time with God, we often find there is also no time during the day. We can go to bed with regret or guilt. Maybe tomorrow, we think. Many times, tomorrow never comes.

When we spend time alone with God at the beginning of each day, we become acquainted with Him and reflect His image in our lives. Throughout our days, the ripple effect of our time with God in the early morning influences the lives of those with whom we have contact.

When these ripples blend with others who spend time

with God, we create mini-waves of love and joy. It all starts with a quiet time and a gentle ripple.

O, God, thou art my God; early
will I seek thee.

PSALM 63:1 KJV

Good Success

E dwin C. Barnes had a burning desire to become a business associate of the great inventor Thomas A. Edison. He didn't want to work for Edison; he wanted to work with him.

As a step toward making his dream come true, Barnes applied for a job at Edison's lab in New Jersey. He was hired as an office worker at a minimum salary—a far cry from a partnership. Months passed with no change in his status or his relationship with Edison. Most people would have given up, feeling their job was taking them nowhere. Barnes, however, stayed on board. He became thoroughly aware of the office environment and each person's job, and he sought out ways to make each person's work more pleasant and efficient. Above all, he remained open and optimistic. He saw all that he did as preparation for the day when he would become a partner with Edison in a joint venture.

The day came when Edison presented the Edison Dictating Machine to his sales staff. They didn't believe it would sell. Barnes, however, saw this awkward-looking machine as his opportunity! He approached Edison, announcing he'd like to sell the dictating device. Since no one else had showed any enthusiasm for it, Edison gave Barnes the chance. He granted him an exclusive contract to distribute and market the office machine throughout America. Barnes succeeded in his goal of working with the great inventor, and achieved his goal to be a success in business at the same time.

Do you have a goal in your mind or heart today? You can be certain you will reach it as you serve others and help them reach their goals. The help you offer to a family member, neighbor, co-worker, or employer today will come back to you in success tomorrow.

Opportunity may arrive in your life today in the disguise of misfortune, defeat, rejection, or failure. See beyond the problems to consider the possibilities. Step out to help someone overcome their difficulties and you may be overwhelmed by the goodness God sends your way!

As we have opportunity, let us do good to all.

GALATIANS 6:10
NKJV

Confidence in the Character of God

"Please understand that there are times when the body, for some reason or another, will spontaneously abort the fetus."

The world seemed to stop dead still for Jim and Donna as they listened to her physician. Donna, in just her fourth month, had begun to hemorrhage earlier in the day. When they came to Dr. Joseph's office, they were concerned; now, they were very frightened.

"It is nothing that you have done or not done," continued Dr. Joseph, "but, we want to send you down for an immediate ultrasound to see how things are doing. I want you to know that if your body has decided to abort the fetus, it is for a good reason. But, let's wait until we know for sure."

With those parting words, Jim and Donna headed to radiology for the ultrasound test silently praying for God's hand of protection on their baby.

"Jim, Jim, can you see the baby? He's right there! He's okay, he's okay!" shouted Donna as soon as the technician showed them the form of their baby on the monitor, and they could clearly see his heart beating. The baby was indeed still alive; Donna's body had not aborted him. They were overwhelmed with relief.

Five months later their first son was born, and another miracle took place as he survived complications during the birth. Upon finally bringing their "miracle boy" home, they both agreed that God must have something special in store for him.

Where had such faith come from? Determined choice, perhaps. As Oswald Chambers once said, "Faith is deliberate confidence in the character of God whose ways you may not understand at the time."[19]

Give your servant a discerning heart.

I KINGS 3:9

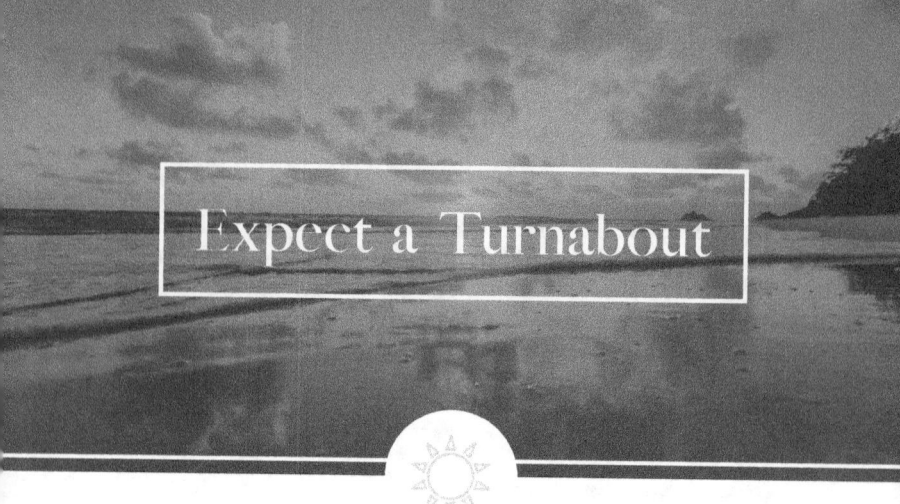

Expect a Turnabout

Our days connect in a unique way according to God's Word. Yesterday's pain, sorrow, and disappointment, as well as yesterday's victories and blessings, become today's agenda.

Were you rejected or alienated by someone yesterday? Then God's agenda for you today is restoration and reconciliation.

Were you struck with sickness or an injury yesterday? Then healing is on today's agenda.

Were you dealt a disappointment or handed a bad report? Then today is a day for hope and good news.

Were you struck with a calamity or disaster? Then today is the time for recovery and rejuvenation.

Did you fail in some way yesterday? Then God's agenda for you today is a second chance!

No matter what worry, frustration, or heartache you took with you to bed last night . . . today holds the hope for a reversal of that "trouble." This is the redemptive nature of God's work in our lives: turning our losses into victories, our sorrow into gladness, and discouragement into reason for praise!

The prophet Isaiah tells us this process results from becoming firmly rooted in God's goodness like great "trees of righteousness." We grow to the point where we see no matter what may strike us on one day, the Lord has a plan for full recovery and more beginning the next. The apostle

Paul echoed this when he wrote to the Romans: "All things work together for good to those who love God, to those who are the called according to His purpose" (Romans 8:28 NKJV).

We never rebound to the point where we began, but He always takes us higher. We are wiser and richer. No matter what hits us, our roots grow deeper, our branches grow longer, and our fruit increases.

Expect God's turnabout in your life today!

Giving them a garland instead of
ashes,
The oil of gladness instead of
mourning,
The cloak of praise instead of a
disheartened spirit.
So they will be called oaks of
righteousness,
The planting of the Lord, that He
may be glorified.

ISAIAH 61:3 NASB

Daily Infusion

Most of us follow established routines each morning to make ourselves presentable for the day. Many of us would never allow certain friends or relatives to see us when we first crawl out of bed. We would rather hide than to have the "real us" exposed before we have showered, shaved, made up our faces and hair, and brushed our teeth.

Although there is nothing wrong with a desire to present ourselves at our best, there needs to also be something on the inside that radiates who Christ is in us.

When a piece of coal is placed on top of a sizzling hot bed of ashes it soon catches the flame and begins to burn in brilliant colors as it radiates heat for long periods of time. However, if we took that same piece of coal away from the flame, it would quickly lose its glow and burn out. The brilliance would disappear and the heat from it would rapidly diminish. Only a big, black, useless lump would remain.

We become useless without a fresh daily infusion of His power and grace. Beginning the day in the presence of the Lord guarantees His light will shine through us before men with brilliance. Sitting at His feet and allowing Him to be our teacher before the day begins provides us with the spark that exposes areas of our lives in which the Lord needs to do His cleansing or healing work.

"Let your light shine before men in such a way that they may see your good works, and glorify your father who is in heaven."

MATTHEW 5:16 NASB

A Broader Perspective

A lthough God gives us a brand-new day every twenty-four hours, we seldom begin it with a brand- new outlook. All too often, we regard the day ahead as "just another day," We may see a different date, but the day seems filled with the same routine, same troubles, same faces, and same responsibilities.

Wouldn't it be wonderful if we could look at each day from a slightly different perspective and, with God s guidance, learn to serve Him better as a result?

A Bible translator named Fraiser learned the importance of different perspectives in a very interesting way. Known simply as "Fraiser of Lisuland" in northern Burma, he translated the Scriptures into the Lisu language. Fraiser continued translation work somewhere else for a time, leaving a young fellow with the task of teaching the people to read.

When he returned six months later, he found three students and the teacher seated around a table, the Scriptures open in front of the teacher. Fraiser was amazed to see that as each of the students read for him, he left the Bible where it was—in front of him. The man on the left read it sideways, the man on the right read it sideways but from the other side, and the man across from the teacher read it upside down. Since they had always occupied the same chairs, they each had learned to read from that particular perspective and each thought that was how their language was written.

When we learn something from only one perspective, we believe it's the only perspective. We have the solution to our problem, but no one else's. Sometimes it's necessary to change seats and assume a different perspective on the same truth in order to help others.

The principles of truth in God's Word never change, but our understanding of them changes. Ask God to give you new insights about Him today. With your new perspective, you may see the solution to a problem that has plagued someone for years.

As our perspective broadens, our ability to help ourselves and others increases.

I have become all things to all men
so that by all possible means I
might save some.

I CORINTHIANS
4:22

A Moment of Truth

With these words, Jean Shepherd introduces a delightful and poignant essay dealing with the trials of adolescence, specifically blind dates:

> There are about four times in a man's life, or a woman's, too, for that matter, when unexpectedly, from out of the darkness, the blazing carbon lamp, the cosmic searchlight of Truth shines full upon them. It is how we react to those moments that forever seals our fate.[20]

In the story, he is fourteen years old and agrees, against his better judgment, to go on a blind date. Contrary to all the logic of blind dates, his date, Junie Jo Prewitt, is beautiful. In fact, she "made Cleopatra look like a Girl Scout." As the evening progresses, however, he becomes aware that Junie Jo is not enjoying the date and in a decisive moment he realizes, "I am the blind date."[21] In this extremely painful moment of truth he realizes he was worried that his date might not be someone he would want to be with, when the truth is he is someone Junie Jo does not want to be seen with.

Shepherd concludes the story with the line: "I didn't say much the rest of the night. There wasn't much to be said."[22]

Life usually presents us with decisive moments— times

when we have no choice but to see ourselves as we really are. In addition, as Shepherd says, "It is how we react in those moments that forever seals our fate."

Moments of truth come each day. When they do, we need to seek guidance and act with humility. For we are only as spiritual as our last decision.

Teach me thy way, O Lord; I will walk in thy truth.

PSALM 86:11 KJV

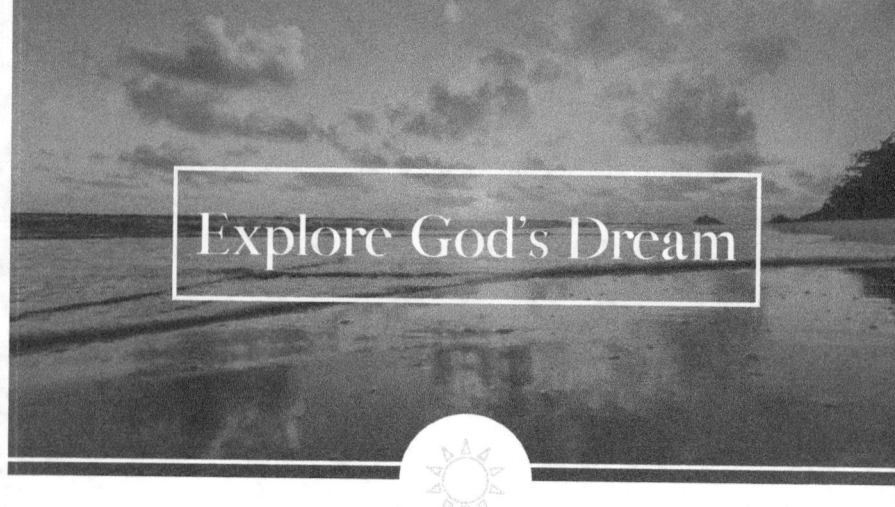

Explore God's Dream

I n *The Reasons of the Heart,* John S. Dunne writes eloquently:

"There is a dream dreaming us," a Bushman once told Laurens Van der Post. We are part of a dream, according to him, part of a vision. What is more, we can become aware of it. Although we are far removed from the Bushmen and their vision, it seems we can indeed come to a sense of being dreamed, being seen, being known. Our mind's desire is to know, to understand; but the desire of our heart is intimacy, to be known, to be understood. To see God with our mind would be to know God, to understand God; but to see God with our heart would be to have a sense of being known by God, of being understood by God.

"If there is a dream dreaming us, it will be God's vision of us, and if we have a sense of being part of that dream, it will be our heart's vision of God."[23]

As we explore and encounter God's dream for us, we find our clearest and highest sense of identity and purpose in life, which gives us motivation and direction for each day.

Do you have a sense of God's vision for your life today? How does He see you? What does He desire for you? What does He dream of you doing, becoming, and being?

We know from His Word God desires for you to be a person of character and quality, a person of noble and

74

uncompromising virtue, a person of strength and spiritual power. He is calling you to a close, personal, and intimate relationship with Him. He eagerly desires to entrust you with His plans and desires for your life.

God has given you specific talents, abilities, spiritual gifts, and material endowments which He longs for you to use to the fullest. Purpose in your heart today to be His friend, His child. His heir, so He can do what He loves to do—reward you with even greater blessings.

The Lord has been mindful of us; He will bless us ... He will bless those who fear the Lord, both small and great.

PSALM 115:12-13
NKJV

Contagious Enthusiasm

"**D**ad, Dad, guess what, guess what," she screamed as she bounded into the room and jumped into her father's lap.

"What? What?" he responded with equal vigor and enthusiasm.

One of the greatest joys of his life was seeing his seven-year-old daughter Crystal's contagious love of life. In fact, she seemed to attack life with a voracious appetite for discovery unknown to him in any other child.

Before she could respond, he remembered a similar time two years earlier when Crystal came home from school with a brochure that described the coral reefs found in the Florida Keys. At that time she could not read yet, but her teacher had read the brochure to the class and she remembered it nearly word-for-word. A couple of weeks later, on a glass-bottom boat ride over the reefs, Crystal delighted everyone on board by identifying the types of coral even before the guide could point them out to the group. She wanted to share her newfound knowledge with everyone.

Shaking him from his reverie, Crystal announced with glee, "My picture won first place in the County Art Fair!" His heart was overwhelmed with joy as he shared in her accomplishment. He was so proud of her. More important, he was so glad that God had blessed his life through Crystal, and he was delighted to hear her news.

God the Father also takes great joy in our accomplishments. Wouldn't it be neat to rush into His presence, jump in His lap, and scream, "Guess what, guess what" whenever we achieve a life goal? Yes, He already knows, but still, He enjoys our thankfulness and loves our enthusiasm.

Let them ever shout for joy.

PSALM 5:11 KJV

Kite Strings

People are often afraid that commitment to Jesus Christ means an endless list of "don'ts" and "thou shalt nots."

Highly motivated personalities are especially vulnerable to the lie that God's ways will restrict their creativity and growth. They fear they may never reach their full potential if they embrace many religious restrictions.

Sadly, some of the smartest people on earth will never reach their full potential because they refuse to accept Jesus. The same holds for those who see His commands as "taking away all their fun." The fact is, true and lasting joy comes through knowing Jesus and following Him.

Consider this: You have watched a kite fly in the wind. Would you say the string that holds it is burdensome? No, it is there to control the kite. The kite will not fly unless it is in partnership with the string. The string and the kite are yoked together. You cannot cut the string and expect the kite to soar right up into the heavens. When the restrictive yoke of the string is cut, the kite may seem to fly freely for a moment, but it will soon crash to the ground.

The string gives the kite direction and purpose by sustaining its position against the wind and using the wind to its advantage. Without the string, the kite would be at the mercy of every passing influence and would doubtless end up being trapped in a tree or falling to the ground. When it is time for the kite to come to earth, the string gently reels it in, safely missing tree limbs and telephone poles.

In like manner, our daily surrender to the Lord Jesus is not burdensome, nor does it take away enjoyment in life. Like the kite string, He makes certain the wind is in our favor and we are always in position to get the most out of life.

Let Jesus be your "kite string" today, and see if you don't fly higher!

My yoke is easy, and my burden is light.

MATTHEW 11:30 KJV

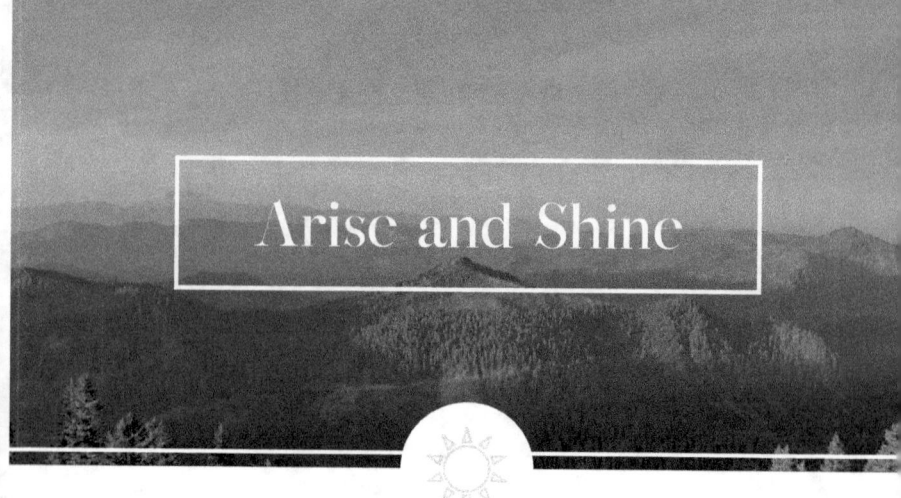

Arise and Shine

While camping deep in the woods, the first sense to attract our attention each morning is . . . smell. The aromatic whiffs of food cooked over an open flame are a wonderful treat to awakening senses. The savory aroma of bacon, sausage, and especially a fresh pot of coffee, gently moves through the forest and rests overhead just long enough to rouse the sleeping camper and produce a memory like no other. Years later campers talk about that experience as if they were reliving it, almost capable of smelling the coffee right then. It's a wake-up call campers fondly cherish.

All of us have moments like these that provide a platform for memories past that are special to us. These classic times of pleasure linger in our minds, much like the smells of a delicious breakfast on a long-ago camping trip. The first call of the morning brings us into the new day and helps to set the pace and tone for the tasks ahead.

Could it be that, as followers of Christ, we experience wake-up calls in our lives that are for more than just reminiscing? Our wake-up calls, lessons learned, and deserts crossed with God's help and presence, can turn these experiences into opportunities that allow God's loving plans for our lives to shine through us to a lost and depraved world.

Isaiah shouted, "Arise, shine!" Share the joy of knowing Christ with others. There are many who will otherwise never awaken to become a child of God unless you share the joy of knowing Christ with them. Become the aroma of Christ.

Arise, shine, for your light has come, and the glory of the Lord rises upon you.

ISAIAH 60:1

Risk and Reward

Perhaps it's been a couple of decades, or maybe only a couple of years since you officially left the nest. Your destination may have been college, a job, or marriage. If your parents were like most, they no doubt were excited, sad, and terrified—all at the same time—at the prospect of your leaving their protective care.

Biologists can relate to those parental feelings, especially when it comes to peregrine falcons. Currently, they are as likely to build their nests on bridges and skyscrapers as on cliffs. When falcon chicks "fledge" in an urban area, they have less room to take practice flights and so their first official flight is sometimes their last. Wires, windows, streets, and sidewalks can be unforgiving landing pads.[24]

To a biologist whose job it is to track these wonderful birds, each lost chick is a devastating blow. However, the chicks will die if they don't attempt flight, and eventually that would mean extinction for the falcons. Risk holds the possibility of failure, but not to risk would mean certain death.

As humans we often spend years preparing ourselves for the future, earning degrees, practicing our craft, seeking out opportunities. Eventually the day comes when we have to face the world, including the possibility for failure.

The thought that we may not succeed at our chosen endeavor shouldn't keep us from spreading our wings. Not only is our own future at stake, but from a much broader perspective, the future growth and development of the human race is involved. Our contribution, even if small, is part of a much greater whole.

As Christians, we must live adventures in faith for ourselves and to further the kingdom of God. However, as children of God, we may falter momentarily, but God assures us of ultimate victory.

If you stumble or make a mistake today, remember who is there to set you back on your feet and get you going again. God has a wonderful, exciting plan for your life (see Jeremiah 29:11) and as long as you follow Him, there is nothing you can do to mess it up!

If the Lord delights in a man's way, he makes his steps firm; though he stumble, he will not fall.

PSALM 37:23-24

Share Your Talents

Satisfaction marked Tony's voice as he spoke of his years in the music industry. "Oh, I could play the trumpet a little bit, and a few other instruments, but as for real talent, I didn't have any. But I do love music and this business."

Over the past thirty years he had been involved with the publication of music and the production of shows in a variety of capacities. According to Tony, the most important decision he ever made occurred when he was a trumpet player in a local orchestra.

"I can remember sitting in the orchestra pit looking up at this young guy who handed some papers to the conductor. They talked for quite a while, and the young guy left." The young man was a music arranger, and Tony said, "That changed my life, because I decided right then and there that I wanted to do the same thing."

Over the next several years, Tony pursued and received his undergraduate degree in music with special emphasis on arrangement. He became a successful professional working for a major music publishing company. Today he serves as a manager and leader in the company. As he nears retirement, Tony obviously loves his chosen profession.

William Jennings Bryan once said, "Destiny is not a matter of chance, it is a matter of choice; it is not a thing to be waited for; it is a thing to be achieved."[25]

Are you at a standstill in your work? Does it feel like a

dead end? Are you feeling restless? Ask the Lord to show you a better way to share your talents with the world. He will surely open new doors for you.

In all labour there is profit.

PROVERBS 14:23
KJV

The Big Audition

A promising singer faced a big audition. Alone in a hotel room far from home, she was excited about the opportunity, but feared failure. *If I don't get this job,* she told herself, *I'll probably never get another audition.*

You may have felt that same way before a job interview, thinking that if you didn't get the job, you might never find another. All of us occasionally fall into the pit of discouragement. We simply can't see any option other than the one before us. The singer dug her way out of that thinking.

On the day of her audition she picked up a magazine at breakfast and read a story about Garry Kasparov, a great Soviet chess player. He had been involved in a monthlong match with Anatoly Karpov, the world champion. Kasparov was losing, but he didn't cave in. He fought hard, regained lost ground, and eventually won the match.

This article inspired the young singer. If he could do it, so can I, she thought. Confidently, she walked onto the stage that afternoon and sang her heart out. That audition led to the first of many jobs. She found new life for her career.

It's easy to lose faith in your ability to succeed. If you look around, you'll find someone else who has triumphed against the odds. Even if you can't find a living example of a failure-reversing or difficulty-overcoming hero in your circle of acquaintances, you can certainly find one in the

Scriptures.

Stories of men and women who faced seemingly insurmountable odds and came through with God's help fill the pages of the Bible. Allow their example to inspire you. The same God who helped them is present and wants to help you now.

"Do not be terrified; do not discouraged, for the Lord your God will be with you wherever you go."

JOSHUA 1:9

Love's Power

Renowned writer Jack London paints an incredible picture of savagery and hope in his work *White Fang*, the story of a wolf dog who is as an outcast at war with a world where only one law exists: eat or be eaten. "There was no soil for kindliness and affection to blossom in. The code he learned was to obey the strong and oppress the weak."[26]

The story boldly tells how the love of one man, Weedon Scott, finally overcomes the fear, hatred, and abuse of a lifetime. In fact, London dubs Scott the "Love Master" because through love and patience he reaches a well deep within *White Fang* and forges an unshakable bond of love and trust.

In some ways this is a projection of London s own life, though the book had a happier ending than London, who died at the early age of forty after a life characterized by many hard times. He never knew who his father was. He worked many different jobs, endured time in jail for vagrancy, and saw his fortune evaporate as fast as he made it. Nevertheless, he never gave up hope, and he was always the romantic at heart.

Commentator Dwight V. Swain states, "In *White Fang*, clearly London is arguing that love is a major—if not the major—civilizing force in a world otherwise ruled by club and fang, brutality and blood."[27]

Be ever mindful of the power of love, even in today's world, which is sometimes ruled by "club and fang, brutality and blood." You will discover ways to be a Weedon Scott in your neighborhood and community. Like London, never give up hope or lose faith in the power of love.

"Do not seek revenge or bear a grudge."

LEVITICUS 19:18

Fruit to Share

Two brothers walked their father's vast acreage when they came upon a peach tree, its branches heavy with fruit. Each brother ate several juicy, tree- ripened peaches.

When they started toward the house, one brother gathered enough peaches for a delicious peach cobbler and several jars of jam. The second brother cut a limb from the tree to start a new peach tree. When he got home he carefully tended the tree cutting until he could plant it outdoors. The branch took root and eventually produced healthy crops of peaches for him to enjoy year after year.

The Bible is like the fruit-bearing tree. Hearing the Word of God is like the first brother. He gathered fruit from hearing the Word and had enough to take home with him to eat later. That doesn't compare with having your own peach tree in the backyard. Memorizing the Word is like having the fruit tree in your backyard. It is there to nourish you all the time.

Scripture memorization is often considered a dull, burdensome task. But we could get highly motivated if we were given one hundred dollars for every Bible verse we memorized! The rewards of Scripture memory may not always be monetary, but they are a far better treasure for life.

One of the greatest values of Scripture memory is that it keeps us from sin. In Psalm 119:11 (NKJV) the psalmist wrote: "Your word I have hidden in my heart, that I might not sin against You."

For many people, the morning is the best time to memorize Scripture because one's mind is fresh, alert, and free from distractions. There are many different ways to memorize Scripture. Find the one that works best for you and begin hiding God's Word in your heart so it may bring continual life and nourishment to you. This will produce fruit in your life, which you can share with others.[28]

Meditate upon these things; give thyself wholly to them; that thy profiting may appear to all.

1 TIMOTHY 4:15
KJV

Ample Supply

S ometimes the only solution for a difficult day is a nice double-dip ice cream cone—that is, if you love ice cream. One fan described a recent trial in ordering her treat at a drive-through window.

She drove up to the speaker to place her order. This ice cream franchise carried too many flavors to list them all on the menu, so customers had to ask if a special flavor was in stock. The attendant answered:

"May I take your order?"

"Do you have butter brickle today?" It was her favorite since childhood and becoming difficult to find.

"No, I'm sorry . . . can we get you anything else?"

Oh, the frustration of drive-through communication. "What else do you have?" she asked.

The attendant paused. "Well . . . what do you want?"

She couldn't help herself. "I want butter brickle!"

It was useless. Determined to find that flavor, she drove two miles to the next franchise store. She approached the speaker with optimism.

"May I take your order?"

"Yes, do you have butter brickle today?"

After a long pause, the attendant responded, "Butter brickle what?"

It is so disheartening to feel that no one hears our needs. How fortunate that God not only understands our every desire, but knows them even before we do. Philippians 4:6

ASV encourages: "In nothing be anxious; but in everything by prayer and supplication with thanksgiving let your requests be made known unto God." In His care we have the assurance our needs will be supplied.

Then shall ye call upon me, and ye shall go and pray unto me, and I will hearken unto you.

JEREMIAH 29:12 KJV

Participate

Management asked a young executive to share with his fellow employees how he felt about participating in the company's voluntary "feed the poor" program. He took one early-morning slot each week to ladle soup and pass out sandwiches to nearly 400 homeless and street people in his city. The young man said this:

I go on Tuesdays to feed those we call poor, and in fact, they are poor in material things. Some of them are poor in many ways, and we try to help them with encouragement, advice, and on occasion, a word of prayer. But in many ways, these hungry and poor men and women have nurtured something in me—they have made me more aware of the spiritual side of my life and they have led me to be aware that we all "feed" each other in many ways every day— either good nourishment for the soul, or poison.

I have a new understanding that when I go home and genuinely compliment my wife, or sit down to read a story to my daughter, or toss a ball with my son, I am feeding something inside them. I no longer see myself as part of the Tuesday-morning feeding team, but as a 24-hour-a-day feeding volunteer.

Who will you feed today?
And what will you feed them?

Mother Teresa wrote in *A Gift for God*, "People are hungry for something more beautiful, for something greater than people round about can give. There is a great hunger for God in the world today. Everywhere there is much suffering, but there is also great hunger for God and love for each other."

Today you will encounter people who are hungry—outwardly and inwardly. God has equipped you in unique ways to "feed" them with natural food as well as His Word, His love, and His presence. He invites you to volunteer to participate in His feeding program.

"Blessed are the poor in spirit, for theirs is the kingdom of heaven."

MATTHEW 5:3 NASB

Capacity for Love

With these words, Mother Teresa explained a lifetime of service:

"I can love only one person at a time. I can feed only one person at a time. Just one, one, one. So you begin . . . I begin. I picked up one person—maybe if I didn't pick up that one person I wouldn't have picked up 42,000."[29]

When she died, an entire world mourned. Sometime before her death, a college professor asked his students to name people they considered truly worthy of the title "world leader." Although many different names appeared on the class list, the one name most commonly agreed upon was Mother Teresa.

"She transcends normal love."

"She has a capacity for giving that makes me ashamed of my own self-centered actions."

"The most remarkable thing about her is that she never grows tired of her work. She never experiences 'burnout' like so many other people. I just hope that I can be as satisfied with my life as she is with hers."

Although none of the students had ever met her, they acknowledged that Mother Teresa had a profound impact on each of their lives by her love. She welcomed the opportunity to fulfill her duties. Can we do any less?

Next time you have a chance to be kind, remember her words: "It is not how much we do but how much love we put in the doing."[30] Isn't it exciting to know that each of us can put enough love into the doing, if we so decide, to be a "Mother Teresa" for at least one other person?

Who knows what would happen if we would all just begin.

Love, joy, peace, patience, kindness, goodness, faithfulness, gentleness, and self-control. Against such things there is no law.

GALATIANS 5:22-23

Creativity

Owning a small business can prove difficult. Just when you start to build a clientele, along comes a crafty competitor who copies your style or improves on your methods. Your revenues begin to fall.

A man on the West Coast found himself in this situation. His first venture was commercial fishing. When larger companies took over the water, he began to rent small sailboats and kayaks to people who wanted to explore the bay. Soon other companies with stronger financial backing moved into his arena.

Once again, he needed a new idea.

How about submarine tours? After doing some research, the entrepreneur realized the cost of buying and maintaining a sub was beyond his reach. But a semi-submersible underwater viewing boat was not! The boat looks like a sub, but it doesn't dive. Passengers can go below deck and view the fascinating world under the sea.[31]

When your income seems to be going out with the tide, you may need to become more creative. Talk with other people, do some research, consider even the "crazy" ideas and glean what you can from them. You never know which wave might be the one that carries you safely and profitably to the shore.

God's creative work didn't end with His creation of the world. He continues His work today through creativity he placed within each of us. He invites us to be part of His plan and purpose for the earth by using this creative energy. Your ideas are God's gift to you for your provision, prosperity, and the fulfillment of your purpose in life.

Ask the Lord to inspire you anew today. Ask Him to give you His next idea for your life!

"See, the former things have taken place, and new things I declare; before they spring into being I announce them to you."

ISAIAH 42:9

Complete Transformation

The parents of a teen struggled with constant calls from their child's school, the youth director at church, and even other parents in the same community, all complaining about the behavior of their fifteen-year-old daughter. Distraught and discouraged, the parents got up early one morning to prayerfully seek the Lord on behalf of their child. They had not been in the habit of praying together or for their children, but found the Lord there for them that morning and every morning after that. Morning prayer time became the one time they longed for during the day.

Encouraged in the rewards of their time in prayer, they also began to read the Bible together. Each day the Lord provided new lessons to teach them. They learned and grew as individuals and as a couple. They noticed positive changes in their daughter's behavior as well. Eventually, what the parents started as a united effort—to cry out for help to the Lord on their daughter's behalf—quickly became a time when the whole family enjoyed together as they gathered for devotions and worship.

When their daughter saw the transformation in her mother and father, she decided to make some changes in her life, too. Today she is a godly young woman who loves the Lord with all her heart.

When we seek the Lord for a specific need, we find He is ready to meet us for all our needs.

I love them that love me;
and those that seek me
early shall find me.

PROVERBS 8:17 KJV

The word *lifestyle* has been popular for several decades. In simplest terms, this word denotes how we live from a financial standpoint, the possessions we choose to buy and how much money we have to spend.

Many books and articles have been written about the simple life—downshifting or downscaling. At the same time, we see an ongoing exaltation in our culture of all that is "excessive." As a nation, we seem to love peering into the lifestyles of the rich and famous. We envy them. Every few minutes, television commercials tell us to buy more and better possessions.

The two paths—one toward a materially leaner life and the other toward a materially fatter life—are like opposite lanes on a highway. We are going in either one direction or the other. We are seeking to discard and downsize, or to acquire and add.

The Scriptures call us to neither a Spartan nor an opulent lifestyle, but rather, to a lifestyle of generosity—a life without greed or hoarding. A life of giving freely, a life of putting everything we have at God's disposal. Our lifestyle is not about how much we earn, what we own, or where we travel and reside. It's how we relate to other people and how willing we are to share all we have with them.

In *Visions of a World Hungry*, Thomas G. Pettepiece

offers this prayer: "Lord, help me choose a simpler life-style that promotes solidarity with the world's poor . . . affords greater opportunity to work together with my neighbors."

As you touch your various possessions throughout the day—from the appliances in your home to your clothing and your vehicle—ask yourself, "Would I be willing to loan, give, or share this with other people?" Then ask the even tougher question, "Do I actually share, loan, or give of my substance on a regular basis to others?"

"For God so loved the world, that he gave."

JOHN 3:16 NASB

Help Another

K evin tells the story of a dear friend and fellow church member who passed away after a long life of love and service.

At the funeral, his children stood up one by one to tell stories about their father, and soon you noticed a recurring theme: that his single most outstanding trait was his willingness to serve others, no matter what the need. He was one of those people who was always ready to lend a hand—to run an errand, do odd jobs, or give someone a ride home. One of his daughters mentioned how everywhere he went, he kept a toolbox and a pair of coveralls in the trunk of his car, "just in case somebody needed something fixed."

More often than not, when we hear the word courage, we think of heroic acts in times of crisis. In our everyday lives, we shouldn't overlook the courageousness of simply being there. Lives change when we faithfully provide for our families, care for the elderly, or lend an ear to a troubled friend. Persistence in making this world a better place to live—for us and others—is definitely a form of courage.

Albert Schweitzer, the great Christian missionary, doctor, and theologian, was once asked in an interview to name the greatest living person. He immediately replied,

"The greatest person in the world is some unknown individual who at this very moment has gone in love to help another."

As you go about your work today, remember that you could be someone else's hero.

Beloved, thou doest a faithful
work in whatsoever thou doest
toward them that are brethren and
strangers withal.

3 JOHN 1:5 ASV

A Task for Jesus

When we think of the noblest professions, we often think of those that offer a service, such as doctors, lawyers, or teachers. Perhaps at the pinnacle of the service professions are those who are involved in full-time ministry—helping others in their spiritual lives in the name of the Lord. We tend to revere most highly those who make a commitment to serving God and others: pastors, priests, monks, missionaries, evangelists, and Bible teachers.

Ministry, however, is not limited to those who earn their living by it. Ministry is the call and challenge of God to all Christians. Ministry is giving to others and living our lives "as unto the Lord.

Ministry happens in the home, in the school, on the street, at the grocery store, in the boardroom, at the committee meeting, and in the gym. It happens wherever and whenever a person, motivated by the love of Jesus Christ, performs an act of loving service for another person.

Someone once wrote:

> *If when we plunge our hand into a bowl of water,*
> *Or stir up the fire with the bellows*
> *Or tabulate interminable columns of figures on our bookkeeping table,*
> *Or, burnt by the sun, we are plunged in the mud of the rice field,*

Or standing by the smelter's furnace
We do not fulfill the same religious life as if in prayer
in a monastery, the world will never be saved.[32]

There is no ignoble work except that which is void of ministry! There is no lack of meaning in any job performed with God's love and "as unto the Lord."

Whatever the tasks you face today, perform them as if you were performing them for Jesus Himself, because ultimately you are!

With good will render service, as
to the Lord, and not to men.

EPHESIANS 6:7
NASB

With the Master

A concert appearance by the brilliant Polish composer and pianist Ignace Jan Paderewski was scheduled in a great American music hall, where the artist was to perform for the social elite of the city.

A young woman waited in the audience with her son for the concert to begin. After sitting for longer than his patience could stand, the youngster slipped away from his mother. The beautiful Steinway piano alone on the stage fascinated him, and he made his way toward it. Before anyone knew what was happening, he crept onto the stage and climbed up on the piano stool to play a round of "Chopsticks."

The audience was horrified. What would the great Paderewski think? The murmurs quickly erupted into a roar of disapproval as the crowd demanded that the child be removed immediately.

Backstage, Paderewski heard the disruption, discerned the cause and raced out to join the child at the piano. He reached around him from behind and improvised his own countermelody to his young guest's "Chopsticks." As the impromptu duet continued, the master whispered in the child's ear, "Keep going. Don't quit, son . . . don't stop . . . don't stop."[33]

We may never play alongside a master pianist, but every day in our lives can be a duet with the Master. What joy it is to feel His love wrapped around us as He whispers, "Keep going . . . don't stop . . . I am with you."

"The Lord your God in
your midst, the Mighty
One, will save;
He will rejoice over you
with gladness, He will
quiet you in His love,
He will rejoice over you
with singing."

ZEPHANIAH 3:17 NKJV

Positioned in Christ

A sheriff decided it was time to tighten the performance standards for his deputies. Each deputy had to re-qualify on the firing range and pass tougher requirements. The target would be moved farther away, from fifteen yards to twenty-five yards, and the deputies were required to fire off twelve shots in eighteen seconds.

The day before trials, Deputy George Burgin was fitted with his first pair of trifocals. George prepared for his shoot and drew a bead on the target to help his aim.

> "Suddenly," he said, "I began to perspire. When I perspire, my glasses fog up. There I was with a bead drawn on the target, and all I could see was fog. Then I remembered what our old Navy instructor had taught us: 'If (for some reason) you ever lose sight of the target,' he said, 'just remember your position.'"

> "So, I just held my position and pulled the trigger as fast as I could. By then I had less than eighteen seconds, but I fired all twelve shots. When I took off my glasses and wiped them, I discovered I had hit the bull's-eye every time."[34]

Sometimes circumstances may cause us to lose sight of our target, or our goal. We do not have a clear sense of where we are headed. If that's the case, we need to do what Deputy Burgin did and remember our position. As Christians, we are securely positioned "in Christ."

Each day we must choose to orient ourselves and face the challenges of the day—whatever they may be. We have the choice to approach the day's opportunities with eager optimism born of faith. When we do, nothing can happen to make us lose sight of our goal. "Positioned" in Christ, we cannot miss!

Your life is hidden with Christ in God.

COLOSSIANS 3:3
NKJV

On a Better Note!

J udy could take the freeway to work each morning and arrive instantly, nerves revved, almost before she is awake, but freeways are ugly. Instead she takes the scenic route around several local lakes and starts her day with mental pictures of sunrises, flowers, and people in various states of running and walking.

Affluence and architecture notwithstanding, she feels that nature is the attraction—a chance for a city slicker to enjoy a little tranquillity. The slower pace gives her the occasion to see a small troop of deer or watch the ducks and geese depart for the winter and return for their spring nesting activities. She recognizes and studies the walkers and joggers who are out regularly at the crack of dawn.

"I don't know if I have a better workday because I sneak up on the job rather than race to it," she muses. "On some mornings, I don't see one thing that nature has to offer because the day ahead refuses to wait for me to get there, and I spend the entire ride making lists of things to do in my head. But I do know that when I take the time to glance at the roses along the way, I feel more fortified, just like our mothers wanted us to be with a hearty breakfast, mittens, and hats."[35]

Taking a few moments to thank God for the glories of creation will make any day start on a better note!

This is the day which the
Lord has made;
we will rejoice and be glad
in it.

PSALM 118:24 NKJV

Infused with Strength

Philip Haille went to the little village of Le Chambon, France, to write about a people who, unlike other villages, had hidden their Jews from the Nazis. He wondered what caused them to risk their lives to do such extraordinary good.

He interviewed people in the village and was over-whelmed—not by their extraordinary qualities, but by their ordinariness. They were not an unusually bright, quick-witted, brave, or discerning people.

Haille looked for possible connections between the citizens' lives to find the reason they had done what no other French town had done. In the end, the author concluded that the one factor uniting them to do good was their attendance at their little church.

Sunday after Sunday they heard the sermons of Pastor Trochme. Over time they became people who knew what was right and obtained the courage from God to do it. When it came time for them to act boldly—as on the day the Nazis came to town—they quietly did what was right.

One elderly woman faked a heart attack when the Nazis came to search her house. She told Haille about her personal dramatic ploy, "Pastor always taught us that there comes a time in every life when a person is asked to do something for Jesus. When my time came, I just knew what to do."

There were two strong beliefs that gave the citizens of this town inner strength of steel. First, they knew their spir-itual strength together in Christ was greater than any foe they faced. Even in times of war, they did not forsake gathering together. Second, they took the Word of God into their hearts in an active way— knowing God would bless them when the principles of their faith were reflected in their behavior.

The strength and courage Haille discovered in the people of Le Chambon was a result of their simple obedience to God—never to stop meeting together to worship and hear His Word. When extreme difficulty came their way, their unity in the faith was a habitual part of their everyday lives.

Thank God today for a church where you can receive strength and courage. If you don't go to church, ask the Lord to lead you to the body of believers just right for you.

Let us not give up meeting together, as some are in the habit of doing, but let us encourage one another.

HEBREWS 10:25

With a Listening Heart

"We've wasted my whole Saturday," moaned John as his father gently woke him.

The plaintive, anguished tone of his voice created an instant reaction in his father and a flash of anger surged upward. It had been a very long day of painting and hanging wallpaper in Mom's new office and Dad was tired. John had worked hard earlier in the day, but as the novelty wore off he became bored and eventually fell asleep on a couch in an adjacent office. Now his dad, Richard, was waking him so that they could head home.

Before Richard could voice the quick retort that formed in his mind, something caused him to pause. In a flash, he saw the Saturday spent working in Mom's new office from an eight-year-old's point of view.

With newfound compassion he responded to his son, "John, I know that Saturday is just about the most important day of the week when you're eight. I appreciate so much your willingness to give up your Saturday to help us get Mom's office decorated. It has been a very long day and I bet that you're tired too. But, I would like to show you how much I appreciate your support by stopping by the video store on the way home so that we can rent a family movie of your choice. What do ya say?"

In response to Dad's caring attitude, John's anguish and despair turned to pride and he quietly said, "You're welcome. Dad. I would like that."

Sometimes, when we listen with our heart and not our ears, love wins and relationships flourish. For as Johann Wolfgang von Goethe said, "Correction does much, but encouragement does more."

Because thine heart was tender.

2 KINGS 22:14 KJV

Gravitational Pull

I n 1969, millions of people watched the televised Apollo II takeoff launching three men into space. Those three men became the first humans to land on the moon. Many remember exactly where they were when they saw astronaut Neil Armstrong take those historic first steps on the moon. We witnessed one of the greatest achievements in history.

One of the remarkable facts about this space trip is that more energy was used in the first few minutes during and after liftoff than during the next several days of traveling half a million miles to the moon. Tremendous energy was needed to break out of the earth's powerful gravitational pull.

Likewise, inertia is hard to overcome in life. We may feel it takes more energy to launch us into the morning than it does for us to go through the day!

Bad habits, past hurts, bitterness, half-hearted commitment, and unconfessed sin can weigh heavy on our hearts, slow us down, or keep us from going upward and onward with the Lord.

"The secret of daily life," says Macrina Wiederkehr, a Benedictine nun, "is there are no leftovers! There is nothing—no thing, no person, no experience, no thought, no joy or pain—that cannot be harvested and used for nourishment on our journey to God."

We may think the loss of a job or a business failure will

prevent us from moving forward in our career. We may be convinced a difficult childhood will keep us from healthy, loving relationships. We may feel that a physical limitation will keep us from true fulfillment, but that is not so in God's kingdom!

Nothing that happens to us is wasted by the Lord. He uses everything for His life-building purposes when we give all our experiences to Him.

This morning, give each weight or encumbrance that drags you down to God. Then watch them become fuel to propel you out of the "gravitational pull" of bad experiences and into the joy of the Lord!

Let us also lay aside every weight
and the sin that clings so closely,
and let us run with perseverance
the race that is set before us.

HEBREWS 12:1 NRSV

Peaceful Obedience and Rest

While on safari, a missionary family stopped for lunch. The children were playing under a tree a distance away from their parents and the other adults on the team. Suddenly the father of one child jumped up and yelled to his son, "Drop down!" and the son did so instantly. Others in the group were shocked to learn that a poisonous snake was slithering down the tree ready to strike the child. It would have meant certain death if the snake had bitten him. Only the father of the child saw the snake.

Many expressed amazement over the instant response of the child to his father's command. The father explained the abiding love he and his son enjoyed had developed from the trust they had in each other. The boy did not question when his dad gave the command; he trusted him and responded accordingly. The missionary father also expected his son to respond to his command.

The peaceful rest that both of them were able to enjoy later that day was evidence of the abiding rest that God has for each of us as we learn to trust Him. Are you abiding in Christ?

God wants to abide in us and He wants us to abide in Him. Abiding comes more easily for some than others. It is not always easy to know what God has planned for us, but we can be assured that whatever it is, He is ready to equip us with what we need to endure and hold on to that place for as long as He wants us there. Abiding starts with trust and ends with complete rest.

"Abide in me,
and I in you."

JOHN 15:4 NASB

Stand Up

Nine-year-old Kevin was upset to learn one of his favorite popsicle flavors was about to be discontinued. What's a kid to do? Fighting City Hall when you're under voting age can seem like a fruitless endeavor.

"But you're a consumer," the boy's mother said. "Yes, you can make a difference. You can start a protest. You can stand up and be counted." Kevin took his mother's advice.

With the help of his cousins, Kevin launched a petition, eventually gathering 130 signatures. The children also constructed picket signs with catchy sayings. Finally, on a rainy January day, Kevin and nearly a dozen family members marched at the popsicle's headquarters.

The company's CEO saw the marchers from the window of his office and invited them inside. He listened to the children's pleas and then explained the company's position. Extensive marketing research had been done, and thousands of dollars had already been spent to present a new flavor. In the end, however, Kevin and his group won the day. The CEO decided to forget the new flavor and grant the petitioners' plea to return the old flavor to the marketplace.

Never give in to the notion that you are too insignificant to lead the move toward a positive change in your world. As a band leader once pointed out in an inspirational speech to a group of students: the smallest person in the band, the head twirler, is the one who is leading us down the street!

The Lord expects each of us to be bold enough to speak His truth whenever the opportunity arises. Sometimes truth is best expressed in conversations, letters, or face-to-face encounters. Sometimes truth may need to be expressed with placards and petitions. In either case, one person begins the process by taking a stand. You can be that person today.

Be strong and of a good courage, fear not, nor be afraid of them: for the Lord thy God, He it is that doth go with thee; he will not fail thee, nor forsake thee.

DEUTERONOMY 31:6
KJV

Never Give Up!

A diamond prospector in Venezuela named Rafael Solano was one of many impoverished natives and fortune seekers who came to sift through the rocks of a dried-up riverbed reputed to have diamonds. No one had been fortunate to find any diamonds in the sand and pebbles in quite some time. One by one, those who came left the site—their dreams shattered and their bodies drained.

Discouraged and exhausted, Solano had almost decided it was time for him to give up too. He had nothing to show for months of hard work. Then Solano stooped down one last time and scooped up a handful of pebbles, if only so he could say he had personally inspected every pebble in his claim. From the pebbles in his hand, he pulled out one that seemed a little different. He weighed it in his other hand. It seemed heavy. He measured it and weighed it on a scale. Could it be?

Sure enough, Solano had found a diamond in the rough! New York jewelry dealer Harry Winston paid Solano $200,000 for that stone. When it was cut and polished, it became known as the Liberator, and it is considered the largest and purest unmined diamond in the world.

You may have been plugging away at a project for weeks, even months or years, without seeing much progress. Today may be the day. Don't give up!

The Scriptures are filled with examples of men and

women who, on the verge of disaster or failure, experienced God's creative work in their lives. Remind yourself . . .

- *God's Word is true.*
- *God can part the sea.*
- *God can heal the incurable.*
- *God can provide water from a rock and manna in the wilderness.*
- *God can conquer your enemies.*
- *God can still deliver from the fiery furnace and the lion's den.*

Persevere in what He has asked you to do today, because your rewards will be more than you can think or imagine!

I will praise you, for you have answered, and have become my salvation.

PSALM 118:21 NKJV

The election results discouraged Bob. He had been absolutely certain that he would be elected state president of the National Community College Honor Society. His college's chapter had successfully been elected president at the state convention and he had played a pivotal role in the campaign. When they met to select one of their members to hold the office, he believed it would be him. He was wrong.

"Well," he reasoned, "there is still the presidency of the local college chapter. I am sure that I will win that."

He was not elected to this office either. Instead, he was elected chapter vice-president. Though disappointed, he did not give up his dream. When the elected chapter president withdrew from college, Bob became the local president. The story does not end there though.

During the next year, Bob asked his chapter members if they would support him in a bid for national president of the entire honor society. The chapter enthusiastically agreed and the next April he was elected national president of the CommunityCollege Honor Society. He had triumphed over thirteen other candidates.

The lesson he learned from this experience is that you never achieve your goals unless you set them high enough. In other words, for Bob it became essential that he raise his expectations for himself when he did not achieve the goal he had set. Originally, he would have been delighted to serve as a state president. Eventually, he was honored to serve as the national president.

He is a living example of Calvin Coolidge's words, "Nothing in the world can take the place of persistence. Persistence and determination alone are omnipotent."

Though he stumble, he will not fall.

PSALM 37:24

Good Morning God

I n *The Grace of Giving*, Stephen Olford gives an account of Peter Miller, a Baptist pastor who lived during the American Revolution. He lived in Ephrata, Pennsylvania, and enjoyed the friendship of George Washington.

Michael Wittman also lived in Ephrata. He was an evil-minded man who did all he could to oppose and humiliate the pastor.

One day Michael Wittman was arrested for treason and sentenced to die. Peter Miller traveled the seventy miles to Philadelphia on foot to plead for the life of the traitor.

"No, Peter," General Washington said, "I cannot grant you the life of your friend. "

"My friend!" exclaimed the old preacher. "He's the bitterest enemy I have."

"What?" exclaimed Washington. "You've walked seventy miles to save the life of an enemy? That puts the matter in a different light. I ll grant your pardon." And he did.

Peter Miller took Michael Wittman back home to Ephrata—no longer an enemy but a friend.

Miller's example of grace and forgiveness flowed from his knowledge of God's sacrifice for the human race. Because God forgave him and sacrificed His Son for him, he found the grace to sacrifice for his enemy. Although most of us know God's grace and love for us is great, sometimes we must be reminded that His love never fails—even when we do!

At the Pan American Games, a United States diver was asked how he coped with the stress of international diving competition. He replied that he climbed to the board, took a deep breath, and thought, "Even if I blow this dive, my mother will still love me." Then he would strive for excellence.

At the beginning of each day, take a deep breath and say, "Even if I blow it today, my God will still love me." Then, assured of His grace and quickness to forgive, go into the day seeking a perfect score!

All have sinned and fall short of
the glory of God, and are justified
freely by his grace.

ROMANS 3:23-24

Connection

The sounds of the delivery room receded to a quiet murmur of post-delivery activities and near-whispered comments between the parents. The father, gowned with a hair net and masked face, leaned forward touching their child cuddled to the mother. She looked down on the baby who was scowling, her eyes tightly shut. With a sense of awe, the mother stretched forth one finger to gently smooth the child's wrinkled forehead. The need to touch her daughter was urgent, yet she was careful.

Developmental psychologists who have examined the process of childbirth and witnessed thousands of deliveries inform us that the need to gently touch one's newborn is a near-universal impulse crossing all cultural boundaries. Obviously, we were created with an innate need to physically connect with our offspring.

In this sense we are very much like God.

In *The Creation of Adam*, one of Michelangelo's famous frescoes that decorate the ceiling of the Sistine Chapel, he portrays the hand of Adam outstretched with a finger pointed. Opposite to it you see the hand of God in a similar pose reaching toward man. The two fingertips are nearly touching. No image more clearly reveals the Father's heart. He is ever-reaching out His hand to touch, with gentleness and love, those created in His own image.

Mothers and God share a common bond then, do they not? Both possess a deep reverence for the life that they have brought into the world. Both yearn to touch those made in their image.

Preserve my life according
to your love.

PSALM 119:88

Tenacity of a Bulldog

Are you in the midst of a frustrating struggle? Before you throw in the towel, remember this story about the bulldog.

A man once owned two very fine bird dogs, and he had spent many hours training them. One day he looked out his window just in time to see an ugly little bulldog digging his way under the fence into his bird dogs' yard. As the dog wriggled under the fence, the man realized it was too late to stop him.

He thought to himself how uneven the fight would be. The poor little bulldog was surely no match for his animals. Snipping, barking, growling—tails and ears flying—the battle raged. When the little dog had had enough, he trotted back to the hole under the fence and shimmied out.

Amazed that none of the dogs looked any the worse for the fight, he didn't give the incident another thought until the next day, when he saw the little bulldog coming down the sidewalk toward the hole in the fence. To his amazement, a repeat performance of the previous day's battle began. And once again, the little bulldog picked his moment to end the fight, left the bird dogs barking and snarling, and casually slid back under the fence.

Day after day for over a week the unwelcome visitor returned to harass his bigger canine counterparts. Then the man was obliged to leave for a week on business. When he returned, he asked his wife about the ongoing battle.

"Battle?" she replied, "Why there hasn't been a battle in four days."

"He finally gave up?" asked the bird dog owner.

"Not exactly," she said. "That ugly little dog still comes around every day . . . he even shimmied under the fe nee until a day or so ago. But now all he has to do is walk past the hole and those bird dogs tuck their tails and head for their doghouse whining all the way. "

Sometimes persistence is the key to success!

Let us not be weary in well doing: for in due season we shall reap, if we faint not.

GALATIANS 6:4

"**D**ad, have you heard of this book?" Cindy asked, showing him a copy of a highly controversial work. Reverend Bill looked up from his desk to respond to his sixteen-year-old daughter.

"Sure, I have, why do you ask?" he replied.

In fact, he knew a great deal about the book. A movie had recently been produced from the book that was causing quite a stir in the Christian community, and many pastors and church members were so upset that they had even picketed the theaters where the movie was showing.

"I was just wondering if it is a good book," Cindy answered.

"Why don't you read it for yourself and then we will talk about it together?"

In that moment, Bill demonstrated a remarkable faith in his daughter, his own parenting, and his God. By inviting her to read and discuss this book, he said that he trusted Cindy to think for herself. Beyond his faith in her, he modeled his faith in God by trusting that her faith would provide guidance as she made decisions.

The single greatest challenge we face as parents is that of letting go of our children the right way and at the right time. Nowhere is this faith challenged more than in the arena of controversial ideas. Yet, we can have confidence that what we have taught them will keep them, for Scripture says, "Train a child in the way he should go, and when he is old he will not turn from it" (Proverbs 22:6).

Bill could trust Cindy because he knew that her entire life had been characterized by learning the Word of God, and now it was time to put that knowledge to the test.

The eyes of the Lord preserve knowledge.

PROVERBS 22:12 KJV

Positive Plus

What we think about determines what we do. Even more important, the Scriptures tell us what we think about shapes our attitudes and how we live our lives. The Greek city of Philippi was one of the places where the apostle Paul had a fruitful ministry. The Greeks were great thinkers. They loved a good debate, a lively conversation about philosophy, or a rousing time of oratory that might trigger the imagination. Paul wrote to the Philippians: "Whatever things are true, whatever things are noble, whatever things are just, whatever things are pure, whatever things are lovely, whatever things are of good report, if there is any virtue and if there is anything praiseworthy—meditate on these things" (Philippians 4:8 NKJV).

It's interesting to note Paul wrote this immediately after addressing three other concerns in Philippians, chapter 4. First, he tells two women who are having an argument to become of "the same mind in the Lord." Paul wants them to be at peace with each other and to rejoice together in the Lord.

Second, Paul tells them to be gentle with all men. That's descriptive of having peace with those who don't know the Lord. And third, Paul advises them not to be anxious or worried about anything, but to turn all their troubles over to the Lord. He wants them to have total peace of mind and heart.

Paul encouraged the Philippians to become God's "peace people" by turning their thoughts toward God's blessings and Word. He makes it very clear what the result will be: "The God of peace will be with you" (Philippians 4:9).

As we look for the good in others, and meditate on the unending goodness of our Creator, we find the path toward peace with others and the peace that passes all understanding in whatever situation we find ourselves.

Thinking right is more than positive thinking—it is living a life filled with God's goodness, wisdom, and mercy!

As he thinks in his heart, so is he.

PROVERBS 23:7
NKJV

Morning Thirst

The need for a refreshing drink when we first wake in the morning is often so strong that we find ourselves anticipating the taste before we ever get a glass in our hands. That thirst is a driving force that nothing else will satisfy.

There is another thirst that needs to be quenched when we first wake up. A thirst we often ignore until it is so great, that everything else in our lives—relationships, our growth as a child of God, our joy, our peace—begins to wither.

Patti did not have running water inside her home when she was a child. Not since then has she known that same level of satisfaction a morning drink of water can give. This was especially true if the water in the house ran out during the night when it was too cold or too stormy for anyone to make a trip to the source outside. Sometimes it was a long, long wait for morning.

There is a source of living water that is available to us any time of the day or night. It never runs out, it never gets contaminated, it never freezes over, and it is always as refreshing throughout the day as it was with the first sip in the morning.

Renowned missionary Hudson Taylor said, "There is a living God. He has spoken in the Bible and He means what He says and He will do all that He has promised." He has promised to quench our thirst in such a way that we will never be thirsty again!

Are you anticipating a drink from God's cup of refreshing living water in the morning? God gives you permission to start sipping right now.

My soul thirsts for God, for the living God.

PSALM 42:2 NASB

A Different Angle

What if I fail? What if I lose? What if he hates me? What if she yells at me? These questions often go through our minds when we face difficult decisions or trying circumstances. If we speak up and say the wrong thing, how will we ever repair the damage? If we act too hastily and then fail, how can we ever look our loved ones in the eye?

An insurance company executive faced these fears soon after assuming a supervisory post. She had realized that many of her employees were paid less than employees in other departments who did the same type of work.

As a new boss, she knew it was risky to challenge upper management. What would they think of her? However, for the sake of her employees she felt compelled to overcome these fears and act on their behalf. How could she do that?

She asked herself a more important question: "What is the worst that could happen if I . . . ?" Someone could get angry—but that would pass. Raises could be refused—but at least she would have tried. She could lose her job—but she was confident God would supply another.

Trusting God for a good outcome and refusing to give in to her fears, she decided to approach upper management about the discrepancies. When she did, they not only took her concern seriously, but began to do something about the problem.

In whatever situation you find yourself, God is with

you to help you sort it out, look at it from different angles, and ultimately see it from His perspective. Then you can act according to His will and trust Him completely for a great outcome.

Today, live your life God's way! Not only will you see tremendous growth and victory, but He will surround your life with favor.

Whatever happens, conduct
yourselves in a manner worthy of
the gospel of Christ.

PHILIPPIANS 1:27

Only the Facts

There was once a man that John Wesley thought of as miserly, therefore he had little respect for him. He felt so strongly about this man that, on an occasion when the man gave only a small gift to a worthy charity, Wesley openly criticized him.

Not long after, the gentleman paid a visit to Wesley. He was surprised to hear that this man—someone whom he assumed was simply greedy—had actually been living on parsnips and water for several weeks. The man told him that, in his past, he had amassed a great deal of debt. Since his conversion, he made a choice to pay off all of his creditors, and therefore he bought nothing for himself and spent as little as possible elsewhere in order to do so.

"Christ has made me an honest man," he said, "and so with all these debts to pay, I can give only a few offerings above my tithe. I must settle up with my worldly neighbors and show them what the grace of God can do in the heart of a man who was once dishonest."

Wesley then apologized to the man and asked his forgiveness.[36]

It's easy to find fault with others when we don't know their circumstances or reasons for their actions It's also amazing how a few facts can forever alter our perception of a situation. When we feel compelled to judge, it's a good time to ask God for wisdom and patience to understand the facts.

He that is void of wisdom
despiseth his neighbour;
but a man of
understanding holdeth his
peace.

PROVERBS 11:12 KJV

No Identity Crisis

E very day the world challenges your identity by trying to tell you who you are—or ought to be—by shaping your desires, telling you what is important, what values you should have, and how to spend your time and resources. What the world is telling you may not be true.

A rancher had been hunting in the mountains of West Texas. Up high on a cliff he came across an eagle's nest. He took one of the eagle's eggs back to his ranch and placed it under one of his hens sitting on her eggs. Eventually the eagle's egg hatched. The mother hen took care of the eaglet along with her baby chicks that hatched at the same time.

The eagle made its home in the barnyard along with the chickens. It ate, slept, and lived just like the chickens. One day an eagle from the nearby mountain swooped down over the barnyard in search of prey. Trying to get her chicks and the eaglet to safety, the mother hen squawked loudly.

As the great eagle swooped low across the barnyard he also let out a harsh scream—a scream made only by eagles. The young chicks heeded their mother's warning, but the eaglet responded to the call of the eagle. He took flight and ascended, following the eagle to the mountain heights.

What does Scripture tell us about who we are as children of God? We are the apple of His eye (Zechariah 2:8); the flock of His people (Zechariah 9:16); a crown of glory in the hand of the Lord and a royal diadem in the hand of our God (Isaiah 62:3); the temple of God (1 Corinthians 3:17). We are heirs of God and joint-heirs with Christ (Romans 8:17). We are kings and priests of our God (Revelation 5:10). We were created to bear His likeness (Genesis 1:27).

Most important, we are God's children (1 John 3:1). We belong to Him and our hearts cry "Abba, Father!" when He calls to us.

Listen for His call today! Find out who you are and what your purpose is from Him, the One who made you!

Because ye are sons, God hath sent forth the spirit of his son into your hearts, crying, Abba, Father.

GALATIANS 4:6 KJV

Marian Wright Edelman, attorney and founding president of the Children's Defense Fund, often speaks of how Martin Luther King had a profound impact on her life. All Americans have been affected by Dr. King's life in some way and few have not heard his famous comment, "I have a dream." But it was not his public persona that had an impact upon her; it was his willingness to admit his fears.

She writes, "I remember him as someone able to admit how often he was afraid and unsure about his next step . . . It was his human vulnerability and his ability to rise above it that I most remember."

She should know about rising above fear and uncertainty because her life was not an easy one, and one wonders just how often she drew strength from the self-honesty and candor of Dr. King.

Ms. Edelman grew up during the days of segregation, one of five children, the daughter of a Baptist minister. She graduated from Spelman College and Yale University Law School and was the first black woman to pass the bar in the state of Mississippi. She is a prolific and gifted writer and has devoted her life to serving as an activist for disadvantaged Americans, especially children.

Hers is an incredible testimony to the belief in helping others to help themselves. She never doubted that she could make a difference. "I have always believed that I could help change the world because I have been lucky to have adults around me who did—in small and large ways."

We have the same opportunity. Will we respond as well as she? Will we help change the world?

Good will come to him who is generous and lends freely, who conducts his affairs with justice.

PSALM 112:5

No Darkness

O nce upon a time a Cave lived under the ground, as Caves have the habit of doing. Jt had spent its lifetime in darkness.

One day it heard a voice calling to it, "Come up into the light; come and see the sunshine."

But the Cave retorted, "I don't know what you mean. There isn't anything but darkness." Finally the Cave was convinced to venture forth. He was amazed to see light everywhere and not a speck of darkness anywhere. He felt oddly warm and happy.

Turnabout was fair play and so, looking up to the Sun, the Cave said, "Come with me and see the darkness."

The Sun asked, "What is darkness?"

The Cave replied, "Come and see!"

One day the Sun accepted the invitation. As it entered the Cave it said, "Now show me your darkness." But there was no darkness!

The apostle John opens his Gospel account by describing Jesus as the Word and as the Light—"the true light that gives light to every man" (John 1:9). It is John who also records Jesus proclaiming, "'I am the light of the world. Whoever follows me will never walk in darkness, but will have the light of life'" (John 8:12).

Jesus made this statement at the close of a feast, just as giant candelabra were extinguished throughout the city of Jerusalem. During the feast these lamps had illuminated the city so that night seemed to be turned to day. "My light is not extinguishable," Jesus was saying, "regardless of the times or seasons."

As this day begins, remember that you take the Light of the world with you; wherever you go and regardless of what may happen during your day, His light cannot be put out.

The path of the just is like the shining sun, that shines ever brighter unto the perfect day.

PROVERBS 4:18
NKJV

A Moment to Pray

Several years ago a television ad focused on a lovely young woman's smiling face. She was looking down and obviously very busy at the task before her, although the ad did not show what she was doing.

At the same time she was busy with this task she was praying. The ad's emphasis was on taking time to pray no matter what else we must do during the day.

As the camera moved away from this young woman's face and down to what she was doing, it became clear that this was a young mother diapering her baby.

What a lovely picture of how easy it is for us to talk with the Lord. Setting a chunk of time aside every morning might not work every day for you, but during each twenty-four-hour day we can creatively find a portion of time that is just for God.

We mutter and sputter,
We fume and we spurt,
We mumble and grumble,
Our feelings get hurt.
We can't understand things,
Our vision grows dim.
When all that we need is:
A moment with Him.[37]

Many of us are so busy during the day, we find it increasingly difficult to set aside a block of time to spend in prayer, not just a quick prayer of thanks, but a time of genuine communication with the Lord.

God wants this time with us and we need it with Him. There are times we can be alone with the Savior, but we need to creatively look for them.

He has made everything
appropriate in its time.

ECCLESIASTES 3:11

A Listening Ear

Frank, like many Christians, had been taught if he truly wanted God to guide his steps each day, he should spend time with Him first thing every morning. He found a copy of a "Through the Bible in One Year" plan and got down to business: three chapters each morning and two each night.

Somehow the inspiration he expected to discover escaped him. He discussed the problem with his friend Carl. Frank said, "I wasn't sure how I would find the time to read the Bible every morning, but I manage to squeeze it in. Sometimes I have to rush through the chapters a little, but I always remember what I've read. You could quiz me on it and I'd get an 'A.' So why do I feel as if I haven't really read it?"

Carl answered, "It sounds to me as if you're reading the Bible the way you would a textbook. If you want to get into the meaning behind the words, pray before you read and ask God to reveal things to you. Instead of looking at the Bible as a reading assignment, think of it as a special meeting time with God—time you set aside to sit down and hear what He has to say to you."

"I get it," Frank said. "I was doing the old 'what's in it for me?' and expecting God to reward me for putting in the time."

"Give yourself more time to read and study," Carl suggested. "Even a few extra minutes can make a big difference.

Just remember: the more time you give to God, the more time He gives back to you. Your day will go much better if you let Him set the pace and listen for what He has to say."

While it is important to read the Scriptures daily, it is far more important to read until you sense in your spirit that God has said something to YOU. Don't be concerned about reading a specific number of verses or chapters. The key is to read with a listening ear.

I delight in your decrees; I will not neglect your word.

PSALM 119:16

Rich in Contentment

A wealthy man spent his days fishing in the lake beside his mansion. Every day, on the same lake he saw a poor man who lived in a rickety shack. The poor man fished with a stick and some string. He sat only an hour or so, rarely catching more than two fish, then went home.

The years passed, and frustrated from too much thinking, the rich man approached the poor man: "Please excuse me, but we've seen each other fishing here for years, and I'm curious. You sit here every day catching only a few fish and then heading home. I couldn't help but wonder why you don't stay longer."

"You see, if you just stayed one or two hours more each day, you could sell your extra fish in town. You could get enough money for a better fishing rod, then catch more fish. You could eventually get a boat and a net. Then with even more fish, you could hire another man and another boat. Soon you would not even have to be on the boats all day; you could have a huge company earning a lot of money. Then, you could easily spend your days fishing alone, for only as long as you would like, doing what you want with no worries."

"But, sir, I don't understand," said the poor man, "that's what I do now."[38]

To be content with the life God has given us is to live the richest life of all.

Godliness actually is a means of great gain, when accompanied by contentment.

I TIMOTHY 6:6 NASB

Morning People

God made both the day and the night and He called both of them good. It seems God also made "morning people," who have their greatest energy level in the morning, and "night people" who are most productive in the late hours. Let's look at some of the joys of being a morning person.

God promised the children of Israel they would see the glory of the Lord in the morning. (See Exodus 16:7.) This promise came to them when they were hungry and in need of bread to eat. God supplied manna every morning until they reached the Promised Land. Like the children of Israel, we too can see the glory of the Lord when we seek Him in His Word. Each morning He provides the nourishment we need for the day.

Another blessing of morning time is it often brings an end to suffering and sadness. (See Psalm 30:5.) Each day brings us a new opportunity to seek God for a fresh perspective on the problems and needs in our lives. When we give every minute and every circumstance of each day to the Lord, we can expect to see His light dawning throughout our day.

There are many examples in Scripture about people who rose early to meet God or to be about doing God's will, among them Abraham, Moses, Joshua, Gideon, Job, and even Jesus. The Gospels tell us that Jesus went at dawn to teach the people who gathered in the temple courts.

The most glorious event of Christianity—the Resurrection—occurred in the early morning. Each morning we can celebrate Jesus' Resurrection as we watch the light of the day dispel the darkness of night.

God called the light day, and the darkness he called night.

GENESIS 1:5 NKJV

Know the Artist

A ll is still as a man sits at his dining room table allowing the pages of a well-worn Bible to slip slowly through his fingers, basking in the peace of the moment. The pages have a comfortable feel, and the soft plop they make as they fall barely disturbs the quiet. Early morning always brings with it a hush of holiness for him. In his mind's eye he remembers another such morning.

The new dawn air is tangy and sharp as he and his brother turn onto a gravel road bordered by wheat fields. Early in the growing season the wheat is about two feet high and a brilliant green. Suddenly the boy catches his breath. From the edge of the wheat field, a ring-necked pheasant comes into view just as a bright ray of sunshine creates a natural spotlight. As if showing off for God Himself, the pheasant stops and strikes a pose.

Time stands still, sound ceases, and God paints an image on the young boy's brain that will remain for a lifetime. The beautiful hues of the pheasant with its shining white collar glistening in the sunshine against the vivid green of the wheat remains sharply etched in his memory. Whenever he relives that day, he experiences anew the presence of God and a supernatural sense of contentment. Slowly the memory recedes, but the presence of God remains.

Sir Thomas Brown said, "Nature is the art of God." All around us are awesome reminders of a big God who created everything in a matter of days. Isn't it great to know the artist firsthand?

You, O Lord, are a
compassionate and
gracious God,
slow to anger,
abounding in love
and faithfulness.

PSALM 86:15

Continue to Build

F ire is a gift of warmth, light, beauty, and utility. Nothing beats a crackling fire on a cold winter's night, and who hasn't enjoyed roasting marshmallows over an open fire? Fire also can be an enemy. Sometimes it destroys the things we love.

On January 29, 1996, a blaze consumed one of Venice's most treasured buildings: the 204-year-dd opera house, La Fenice. Hundreds of Venetians stood and watched as the building went up in flames.

Cause for sadness? Definitely. Cause for despair? Absolutely not. The construction of La Fenice had been delayed by fire in 1792. Another fire in 1836 had forced the Venetians to rebuild. And after the fire in 1996, Venetians are once again faced with the task of rebuilding their opera house.

Interestingly, La Fenice means "the phoenix," referring to the mythological Egyptian bird that died in a fiery nest, only to emerge from the ashes as a brand-new bird. It is in that spirit the Venetians rebuild.

We can sometimes restore what the fires in our lives destroy. If we desire to rebuild and we truly believe it is what the Lord would have us do, we put our full effort into the task. At other times when the Lord brings us through a fire, He desires the old to be left in ashes so something entirely different can be constructed on the site. This is true not only in the physical world in which we live, but also in the interior world of our souls, when our inner mettle is "tried by fire."

In those cases when we can't or shouldn't rebuild, we can remember Shadrach, Meshach, and Abednego. They were thrown into Nebuchadnezzar's fiery furnace for refusing to bow to an idol. (See Daniel, chapter 3.) Like them, we can emerge stronger and better after the test. We can see our lives touch and inspire others by standing up for what we believe.

If you are facing calamity or disaster today, the Bible tells you to quickly put it behind you by rebuilding or building something new. Whichever God desires, you will become stronger and better than before if you "press on!"

Forgetting what is behind and straining toward what is ahead, I press on toward the goal to win the prize for which God has called me heavenward in Christ Jesus.

PHILIPPIANS 3:13-14

Do you ever feel inadequate? Unworthy? Most of us do from time to time. And we all know people who we think are too successful to have those same feelings.

Martin Luther, the sixteenth-century German preacher and Bible scholar who initiated the Protestant Reformation, sounds like the type of man who would be eminently sure of himself. Any man who would dare to publicly question the theology of his church—in a time when it could cost him his life—could not be a man who had doubts about himself. Or could he?

In truth, Luther spent his early years obsessed by his presumed unworthiness. He periodically fasted and mistreated his body in an attempt to "earn" God's favor. On a pilgrimage to Rome, he climbed the Steps of Pilate on his knees, kissing each step. He wrote later that in those years he was constantly confessing his sins to God, yet he never felt he had done enough.

While reading the book of Romans, Luther realized he could not earn his salvation. The Bible says we receive salvation, we do not earn it. (See Romans 4:13-14.) Those verses of Scripture liberated Luther, radically changing his opinion that it was his works which made him worthy of God's grace.

He recognized Jesus Christ had already done all the "earning" necessary for his salvation. He simply needed to receive what Jesus had done—that He had paid the price for his sin on the cross—by faith.

On days when we fall flat on our faces in failure or just feel low, we need to remind ourselves that our mistakes are not the end of the world. Our inadequacy is not our doom. Our salvation doesn't depend on how well we manage to color inside the lines!

Perfection may be our aim, but when we realize we haven't arrived there, we need to relax and turn to the Lord, saying, "Forgive me for what I have done, and for what I have left undone. I trust You to be my Savior, my Deliverer, my Hope, and my Perfection." He is and He always will be!

"It will come about that whoever calls on the name of the Lord will be delivered."

JOEL 2:32 NASB

Give Yourself

B ritish statesman and financier Cecil Rhodes, whose fortune acquired from diamond mining in Africa endowed the world-famous Rhodes Scholarships, was known as a stickler for correct dress—but not at the expense of someone else's feelings.

Once it was told that Rhodes invited a young man to an elegant dinner at his home. The guest had to travel a great distance by train and arrived in town only in time to go directly to Rhodes' home in his travel-stained clothes. Once there, he was distressed to find that dinner was ready to begin and the other guests were gathered in their finest evening clothes. But Rhodes was nowhere to be seen. Moments later, he appeared in a shabby old blue suit. The young man later learned that his host had been dressed in evening clothes, but put on the old suit when he heard of his guest's embarrassment.[39]

Rabbi Samuel Holdenson captured the spirit behind Rhodes' gesture, saying:

> *Kindness is the inability to remain at ease in the presence of another person who is ill at ease, the inability to remain comfortable in the presence of another who is uncomfortable, the inability to have peace of mind when one's neighbor is troubled.*

The simplest act of kindness not only affects the receiver in profound ways, but brings blessings to the giver as well. It makes us feel good to make others feel good. So do something nice for yourself today—commit a random act of kindness!

In your godliness, brotherly kindness, and in your brotherly kindness, love.

2 PETER 1:7 NASB

Reward

Our society is inundated with hundreds of reasons why being first is a goal to be obtained. It is necessary to be first in every line to get the best seat. Winning first place carries the most weight, the largest purse, and the most recognition. Rarely are we able to recall the second runner-up in any event. No doubt about it, first is the creme de la creme. Or is it?

There is nothing wrong with obtaining first place status. The Bible encourages us to set high goals and reach for them with perseverance. Each of us knows people we admire because of the goals they have set and reached through committed determination. But what about those who do their very best and never make the first string, never get the top grade, never win the trophy, etc.? What do they do with God's promises?

God has a plan for each of us. The stakes are often very high. The game plan will be interrupted many times by the devil. We will doubt, be discouraged, and face what seem to be impossibilities. However, God promises us that if we seek Him first, we have whatever we need—all of His blessings and all of His promises.

It takes faith! Some never make it to the finish line, yet their labor is rewarded because they did their best. The contributions of those on the sidelines or behind the scenes are rewarded, although not with a shiny plaque they can display.

Each of us can place first if we simply believe the promises of God and become dead to doubt, dumb to discouragement, and blind to impossibilities.

"Seek first His kingdom
and His righteousness;
and all these things shall
be added to you."

MATTHEW 6:33 NASB

Embrace Your Day

The sun is barely up and that annoying alarm clock is blaring in your ear. Groggily you reach over and fumble around until you hit the snooze button. *Just a few more minutes,* you think, *and then I can get up and face the day.*

The alarm sounds again. You know you can't put it off any longer. It's time to face the inevitable. It's time to wrestle another day to the ground.

After a couple of cups of coffee, your brain is finally humming. Now the question is, which of today's tasks should you tackle first? Before you begin your work, you might seek inspiration from this prayer, written by Jacob Boehme, a German shoemaker who was born more than 400 years ago:

Rule over me this day, O God, leading me on the path of righteousness. Put your Word in my mind and your Truth in my heart, that this day I neither think nor feel anything except what is good and honest.

Protect me from all lies and falsehood, helping me to discern deception wherever I meet it. Let my eyes always look straight ahead on the road you wish me to tread, that I might not be tempted by any distraction.

And make my eyes pure, that no false desires may be awakened within me.[40]

A day without distractions,
focused only on the important.
A day viewed through pure eyes.
A day marked by goodness and honesty.
A day of clear direction and no deception.
A day without falsehood and lies.
A day in which God's Word rules our minds
and His truth reigns in our hearts.

Now that's a day worth getting up for! That's a day worth embracing fully, from the first second.

"It is God who arms me with strength and makes my way perfect."

2 SAMUEL 22:33

Getting yourself out of bed in the morning is one thing. Feeling prepared to face whatever comes your way that day is another. Where do you turn for a confidence-booster? Believe it or not, one of the best confidence-builders you can find may be inside those fuzzy slippers you like to wear: your own two feet.

Researchers have discovered that regular exercise—thirty minutes, three or four times a week—boosts the confidence level of both men and women. This is due in part to the way exercise strengthens, tones, and improves the body's appearance. It also has to do with brain chemistry.

When a person exercises, changes take place inside the brain. Endorphins, released as one exercises, are proteins that work in the pleasure centers of the brain and make a person feel more exhilarated. When the heart rate increases during exercise, neurotrophins are also released, which cause a person to feel more alert and focused.

Are you feeling anxious about your day? Take a walk, jog, cycle, or do some calisthenics first thing in the morning. See if you don't feel a little more on top of the world.

Those who exercise regularly also feel that if they can discipline themselves to exercise, they can discipline themselves to do just about anything!

The human body is one of the most awesome examples of God's creative power—an example we live with daily.

He has created us not only to draw confidence from reading His Word and experiencing His presence through prayer, but also from the use of our body.

Put on those walking shoes and talk with God as you go! Not only will your body become more fit and your mind more alert, but the Holy Spirit will give you direction and peace about your day.

God did not give us a spirit of timidity, but a spirit of power, of love and of self-discipline.

2 TIMOTHY 1:7

The Morning Report

W hether on the radio by the bed, the TV set next to the breakfast table, or the car stereo, the morning news is part of the vast majority of households in our nation. While we decry the negative message of most news items, we seem addicted to hearing more and more news. The result: we allow more and more negativism into our national psyche. If we add feature programs that claim to be "informative" about human nature—including sensational talk-show programs—we only increase the negative influence on our lives.

The Gospel shines in sharp contrast.

The word *gospel* is derived from an early Anglo-Saxon word *godspel.* It meant "good tidings" and later took on the meaning "God-story," or the story of God's love shown to us through the sacrifice of His Son, Jesus Christ. The Gospel is good news.

How do we shine the light of the Gospel on the darkness of the world's news reports? One way is to proclaim the goodness of Jesus Christ every time we hear a negative report.

Is the report about crime? Then we proclaim, "Jesus can change the hearts of the most hardened criminals. He can heal the wounds of those victimized. Even so, have mercy, Lord Jesus."

Is the story about racial tension, war, or a conflict among ethnic groups? Then we proclaim, "Come, Lord

Jesus. Be the Prince of Peace in this situation."

Is the news story about sickness, disease, or epidemic? Then we proclaim, "Jesus is the Healer. Make us whole, Lord Jesus."

Is the story about a natural catastrophe, storm, or accident? We proclaim, "Jesus calms the storms and brings about good from evil. Come and reign, Lord Jesus. Renew us with Your life."

Even if we stop watching negative television programming and try to avoid anything ungodly, we will still hear negative news and encounter difficult circumstances. However, when we hear a bad report, we can counteract it with a good word about the Lord Jesus Christ, our Good News. He is the best news report any person can ever hear.

Thus says the Lord: Sing aloud
with gladness for Jacob, and shout
for the head of the nations . . .
Proclaim, praise, and say, The Lord
has saved his people.

JEREMIAH 31:7 AMP

Invitations

Rita stood on the sidewalk peering wistfully at the beautiful home. Through the curtained windows she saw nicely dressed people chatting with one another and enjoying refreshments. She clutched an engraved, personal invitation to the dinner party in her hand. Her professor, impressed with her academic abilities, had invited her to attend this evening's affair so that she might meet others at the university.

She carefully fingered the invitation, looked down at her party dress which seemed dull and ordinary in comparison to the gowns she saw through the window. With a sadness of the soul she turned and slowly walked away. Clutched between her fingers: the unused invitation.

This poignant and painful scene from the British movie *Educating Rita* demonstrates just how difficult it is for one to accept the possibility of a new life. Rita came from a lower middle class family, and no one had attended university before her. She struggled with feelings of inadequacy and was forever wondering how she would "fit in." It is this sense of self-doubt that caused her to fail to take action on the invitation.

However, thanks to a persistent professor, who saw more in her than she saw in herself, she eventually accepted his invitation to join a new world. By the movie's end, this once modest woman excels as a scholar.

The invitation to become and then excel as a Christian

is for each of us. The greatest joy, though, is in knowing that our Master Teacher always sees much more in us than we usually see in ourselves.

God does not ask about our ability, but our availability.

The son said unto him, Father, I . . .
am no more worthy to be called
thy son.

LIKE 15:21 KJV

Make It Count!

Most of us can look around and find reminders of good intentions. We readily see areas where we never followed through to reach a goal. The seldom- used exercise equipment needs dusting. A piano, intended to fulfill our dreams of happy family sing-a- longs, sits silent.

The books piled on the nightstand remain to be read. The laptop computer we intended to take on vacation to write a novel is still in its original packaging. More important, there are the children in our family who wait for our attention. Every child has gifts and abilities waiting to be developed and that takes time.

To tap into potential takes intentional, concerted effort. It doesn't just happen. Time for meaningful interaction and activity doesn't always appear to us as we juggle a full day of appointments and other commitments.

The time God gives to us is ours to spend and we determine how to use it. We can fill it with life- building activities, or we can let it sift through our fingers hour by hour, day by day, week by week, until before we know it, an entire year is gone and very little is accomplished.

As long as you are alive, your time—24 hours, 1,440 minutes, 86,400 seconds a day—will be spent. It is up to you to decide how you are going to spend it.

Accept the challenge to make every moment count! When you take your child to the dentist, make it an adventure, a time to listen, learn, and share God's wisdom. Is there a free hour when you can sit quietly and read a chapter or two in one of those books?

Look at what you have planned for today and set your priorities according to the goals you have set for your life. Do the same thing tomorrow and the next day. It won't be long before your life will begin to be more productive and more fulfilling.

While it is daytime, we must continue doing the work of the one who sent me. Night is coming, when no one can work.

JOHN 9:4 NCV

Breakfast Guest

It was at sunrise when the men returned from an all night fishing trip, and they had nothing to show for their efforts. Not a single fish. As the boat approached the shore, the men noticed a man calling to them. He wanted to know if they had any fish.

The tired fishermen answered that they did not. The man then told them to cast their nets on the right side of their boat. When they did as the man on the shore suggested, the net immediately filled with large fish.

One of the fishermen was John, a disciple of Christ. He recognized the man on the shore. It was the Lord. The disciples knew Jesus because they had spent time with Him. They recognized Him from a distance. When the disciples reached shore Jesus had a charcoal fire already laid with fish cooking and bread ready. He invited the disciples to bring more fish from their catch and join Him for breakfast.

Can you imagine having breakfast with Christ? Think of what it would be like to have Christ sitting across from you at your breakfast table. What kind of preparations would you make? What would you wear? Who would you tell? What would you serve? Would you be on "pins and needles" getting ready, wanting everything to be perfect?

Christ is ready with an RSVP to pass back immediately upon our invitation to Him. He is delighted to join us for breakfast, or any meal—anytime!

"Come and have breakfast."

JOHN 21:12 NASB

Grow Deep

A writer for a local newspaper interviewed a farmer about the effects of recent weather on his crops. Rain had been abundant and the farmer's soybean and corn crops were tall and lush.

"My crops are especially vulnerable right now," said the farmer. This statement took the reporter by surprise. He had planned to focus his article on the good harvest expected and the economic boom it would bring for the town.

The farmer went on, "Even a short drought could have a devastating effect."

"Why?" asked the reporter.

The farmer explained that while we see frequent rains as a benefit, during rainy times the plants are not required to push their roots deep in search of water. The roots remain near the surface, leaving the plants unprepared for drought.

His crop also faced the danger of sudden strong wind storms. Again, because of the shallow root structure, a strong wind could wipe him out in only a few minutes.

Some Christians enjoy an abundance of rain showers that come in the form of praise services, fellowship with other believers, and times of rich Bible teaching. But when stress enters their lives, these same Christians can lose faith, abandon God, or believe God to be unfaithful. Why? Their roots have never pushed much below the surface.

Their spiritual life is top-heavy, relying on others more than on personal devotion in prayer and study of God's Word. They are especially vulnerable to the strong winds of adversity or the searing heat of stress.

Only the roots grown deep into God will help us endure tough times. Put your roots down more deeply today. Spend time with the Lord . . . in the Word . . . and on your knees.

Just as you received Christ Jesus as Lord, continue to live in him, rooted and built up in him, strengthened in the faith as you were taught, and overflowing with thankfulness.

COLOSSIANS 2:6-7

Heart Song

S inger and songwriter Bobby Michaels tells how one summer he sensed a growing hunger to come up with a new song, but he could not find it within him. As he visited his publishing company to discuss a new album, he met a young man working as an intern.

The young man mentioned that he wrote songs, and Bobby found himself pouring his heart out to the young man.

"Forget what might be appealing or what might sell," said the young man. "Just tell me what you think God wants you to sing about." Bobby's story inspired the young man to write a beautiful song that uncannily communicated Bobby's heart. The name of the song is "My Redeemer Is Faithful and True." It is an unpretentious and simple prayer of thanksgiving to our Creator. It is a reverent statement of faith in God's faithfulness. It literally made Bobby's heart sing anew his love for his Savior.

The sales staff and editors did not like the song. In fact, they did not believe that it would sell. "Too slow," they said. "Too redundant." On and on they went, but Bobby remained adamant that this song was directly from God and that it was anointed of God. It ministered to him, and it would minister to others.

Bobby was right. God has used the song to bless count-less numbers of individuals, and the testimony he gives at his concerts prior to singing the song makes thousands of hearts sing right along with him. Steven Curtis Chapman is the young man who wrote the song, a talented writer and winner of numerous Dove and Grammy awards.

God is simply amazing! What new song does He want to put in your heart today?

He put a new song in my mouth, a hymn of praise to our God.

PSALM 40:3

Do it Differently

Sometimes our daily routine seems more like a never-ending rut. The activities and responsibilities that were once fresh and new gradually become stale and old. What can you do to shake things up a bit?

A woman asked herself that question one morning. She had done all she needed to do to get her children off to school and her husband to work. Now she was home alone, looking for the motivation to face her day.

She said to herself, *I know what I'll do. I'll turn things upside-down. Instead of sticking to my usual schedule, I'll reverse the order.*

That meant her first item of business was preparing dinner. She thought she might feel strange preparing meat and vegetables at 9am, but she was surprised to find she felt a sense of relief at having this "chore" done early. Somehow, it made the rest of the housework and errands less stressful.

She found a little extra time to write a letter and catch up on some reading, and by the time her children came tromping in from school, she felt happier than she had in weeks. She was already thinking of other ways to add variety to her daily routine.

Who says you have to do the same things in the same way at the same time every day?

The Bible clearly tells us that our God is a God of

infinite variety! While His commandments are not nego-tiable, His methods often change. That's part of His nature as our Creator. The Lord is continually creating new meth-ods to reach us with His love and to show us His care.

Break out of your rut today! Ask the Lord to give you insight into how you might participate more fully in His creative process by doing things differently.

Gird your minds for action.

1 PETER 1:13 NASB

The Face of God

Dutch psychologist and theologian Henri Nouwen was known for his determination to break down barriers, whether between Catholic and Protestant or therapist and patient. He spent most of his life pursuing a high-pressure career as a sought-after speaker and author.

Years of travel and dozens of books took such a toll on his health and spirit that he eventually retreated to Toronto, Canada, to become priest-in-residence at Daybreak, a home for the severely disabled.

Nouwen lived a quiet life at Daybreak, residing in a small, simple room, and ministering to the patients at the facility. He had a special relationship with a resident named Adam, a profoundly retarded young man unable to walk, talk, or care for himself. Nouwen devoted nearly two hours every day to caring for Adam—bathing, shaving, combing his hair, feeding him.

To onlookers, it seemed a great burden on the priest to spend so many hours on such menial duties. When asked why he spent his time in this way, Nouwen insisted he benefited from the relationship. He described how the process of learning to love Adam, with all of his incapacities, taught him what it must be like for God to love us, even with all our frailties.

Ultimately, Henri Nouwen concluded "the goal of education and formation for the ministry is continually to recognize the Lord's voice, His face, and His touch in every person we meet."[41]

Have you seen the Lord's face lately?

No one has beheld God at any time; if we love one another, God abides in us, and His love is perfected in us.

1 JOHN 4:12 NASB

The Full Picture

I f you have ever worked a complicated jigsaw puzzle, you know three things about them. First, they take time. Few people can put several hundred pieces of a puzzle together rapidly. Most large and complex puzzles take several days, even weeks, to complete. The fun is in the process, the satisfaction in the accomplishment.

Second, the starting point of a puzzle is usually to identify the corners and edges, the pieces with a straight edge.

Third, jigsaw puzzles are fun to work by oneself, but even more fun to work with others. When a "fit" is discovered between two or more pieces, all the participants feel the excitement.

Consider the day ahead of you like a piece in the jigsaw puzzle of your life. Indeed, its shape is likely to be just as jagged, its colors just as unidentifiable. The meaning of today may not be sequential to that of yesterday. What you experience today may actually fit with something you experienced several months ago, or something you will experience in the future. You aren't likely to see the big picture of your life by observing only one day. Even so, you can trust that there is a plan and purpose. All the pieces will come together according to God's design and timetable.

On some days, we find straight-edged pieces of our life's puzzle—truths that become a part of our reason for being. On other days, we find pieces that fit together so we understand more about ourselves and about God's work in our lives. On all days, we can know the joy of sharing our lives with others and inviting them to be part of the process of discovering who we are.

The main thing to remember is to enjoy the process. Live today to the fullest, knowing one day you will see the full picture.

Looking away [from all that will distract] to Jesus, who is the leader and the source of our faith [giving the first incentive for our belief] and is also its finisher [bringing it to maturity and perfection].

HEBREWS 12:2 AMP

Limitless Possibilities

Many centuries ago, a young Greek artist named Timanthes studied under a respected tutor. After several years of effort, Timanthes painted an exquisite work of art. Unfortunately, he was so taken with his painting that he spent days gazing at it.

One morning, he arrived to find his work blotted out with paint. His teacher admitted destroying the painting, saying, "I did it for your own good. That painting was retarding your progress. Start again and see if you can do better." Timanthes took his teacher's advice and produced Sacrifice of Iphigenia, now regarded as one of the finest paintings of antiquity.[42]

Timanthes' teacher knew what many great artists know—we should never consider ourselves truly finished with our work.

When the legendary Pablo Casals reached his ninety-fifth year, a reporter asked, "Mr. Casals, you are ninety-five and the greatest cellist who ever lived. Why do you still practice six hours a day?" And Casals answered, "Because I think I'm making progress."

Maya Angelou applies that same logic to daily life. In her book, Wouldn't Take Nothin' for My Journey Now, she writes: "Many things continue to amaze me, even well into the sixth decade of my life. I'm startled or taken aback when people walk up to me and tell me they are Christians. My first response is the question 'Already?' It seems to me

a lifelong endeavor to try to live the life of a Christian . . .
"43

How exciting it is to be a work in progress. With God
s help, our possibilities are limitless!

We are His workmanship, created
in Christ Jesus for good works,
which God prepared beforehand
that we should walk in them.

EPHESIANS 2:10
NKJV

Destined for Greatness

I t was built for an international exposition in the last century and both critics and citizens called it monstrous. They loudly demanded the structure be torn down as soon as the 1889 exposition closed. Yet from the moment its architect first conceived the structure, he took pride in it and loyally defended it. He knew it was destined for greatness.

Today it stands as one of the architectural wonders of the modern world. It has become the primary landmark of Paris, France. The architect was Alexander Gustave Eiffel. His famous structure? The Eiffel Tower.

Jesus Christ was loyal to another structure—the Church. He entrusted the building of the Church to an unlikely band of disciples, whom He defended, prayed for, and prepared to take the Gospel to the far-reaching corners of the world. To outsiders, the disciples of Jesus probably had a reputation as ignorant, politically weak, religiously untrained, disorganized, and in moments, blundering idiots. But Jesus, the architect of the Church, knew His structure was destined for greatness.

Being a Christian has never been "politically correct." Critics through the years have compiled a list of derogatory names to call the Church and its members. In spite of criticism, however, we are instructed to carry on. We are to persist in building the body of Christ until His return. As we build, we are assured we will please God and He will bless us.

The famous Finnish composer Jean Sibelius once consoled a young musician who had received a bad review by saying, "Remember, son, there is no city in the world where they have erected a statue to a critic."

Jesus said, "'I will build my church; and the gates of hell will not prevail against it'" (Matthew 16:18). One day the Church will be the ones left standing. What will the critics say then?

No matter what comes your way today, be proud you are a member of Jesus' Church!

"Blessed are you when people insult you, persecute you and falsely say all kinds of evil against you because of me. Rejoice and be glad, because great is your reward in heaven, for in the same way they persecuted the prophets who were before you."

MATTHEW 5:11-12

The Sunrise

Sunrise, shining its beams through the window on a cold winter's morning is a welcome sight. Even if the air outside is icy cold, sunrise gives the illusion of warmth. With the rising sun, the city opens its shutters and prepares for the day. In the country the farm animals are let out to pasture. Kids are off to school, adults are on their way to work, and each has a different perspective of the sunrise.

Sunrise happens whether we see it or not. Clouds may cover the sky completely and we are unable to experience the beauty of the sunbeams as they make their way to the earth. No matter what the climate, the sun still rises in the eastern horizon and sets over the west. Sunrise is on God's clock, and it is ours to enjoy in the early mornings when we can see it clearly. It is just as much there for us to enjoy when the cloud shadows cover it. We can trust it to be there—although it may be hidden for a while.

We can also trust God to be there every morning because He is the one, irrefutable reality in this life, and He remains constant and true!

GOOD MORNING, GOD

Life is a mixture of sunshine and rain,
Laughter and teardrops, pleasure and pain—
Low tides and high tides, mountains and plains,
Triumphs, defeats and losses and gains.
But there never was a cloud
That the Son didn't shine through
And there's nothing that's impossible
For Jesus Christ to do!

Helen Steiner Rice

"The sunrise from on high shall
visit us."

LUKE 1:78 NASB

Regular, frequent prayer is an important part of the lives of people who desire a meaningful relationship with God. John Wesley, a devout Christian and the founder of Methodism, had a deep concern for the "state of his soul." That concern caused him to pray regularly two hours a day. Here is one of John Wesley's prayers, which you may want to include in your devotions:

O God, who are the giver of all good gifts, I your unworthy servant entirely desire to praise your name for all the expressions of your bounty toward me. Blessed be your love for giving your Son to die for our sins, for the means of grace, and for the hope of glory. Blessed be your love for all the temporal benefits which you have with a liberal hand poured out upon me; for my health and strength, food and raiment, and all other necessaries . . . I also bless you, that after all my refusals of your grace, you still have patience with me, have preserved me this night, and given me yet another day to renew and perfect my repentance.

Make yourself always present to my mind, and let your love fill and rule my soul, in all those places, and companies, and employments to which you call me this day. O you who are good and do good, who extend your loving-kindness to all mankind, the work of your hands, your image, capable of knowing and loving you eternally: suffer me to exclude none, O Lord, from my charity, who are the objects of your mercy; but let me treat all my neighbors with the tender love which is due to your servants and to your children. Let your love to me, O blessed Saviour, be the pattern of my love to them.

Preserve my parents, my brothers and sisters, my friends and relations, and all mankind in their souls and bodies. Forgive my enemies, and in your due time make them kindly affected toward me. O grant that we, with those who are already dead in your faith and fear, may together partake of a joyful resurrection.[44]

Let me hear of your steadfast love in the morning, for in you I put my trust. Teach me the way I should go, for to you I lift up my soul.

PSALM 143:8 NRSV

Sensitivity

On the Big Island of Hawaii a delicate little plant called Sensitivity grows, a member of the Mimosa family. Its name is derived from the movement it makes when anything, including a change in the wind, comes near or across it. This minute, spiny stemmed tropical American plant, grows close to the ground. Unless you are directly upon it, you can't distinguish it from grass or weeds in the same area and it can easily be crushed underfoot.

As the sun rises in the South Pacific, the tiny Sensitivity plant opens itself as wide as it can and reaches upward toward the warmth of the early morning sunbeams shining down from heaven. This wee drooping plant has a built-in mechanism that causes it to quickly fold itself over and withdraw from anything that might cause it harm. However, Sensitivity can't distinguish between a lawn mower rolling toward it to cut it down, or the man coming by to make certain it is protected.

Each of us has a built-in need to protect ourselves from danger and those who would harm us. God gave us His Word as a manual to equip us to be aware of the ways of the enemy and to prepare us to know how to protect ourselves.

We can reach up every morning, even when it's raining or snowing, and receive His warmth, His love. His protection, and His anointing for the day ahead of us. God has blessed us with His sensitivity, but we must be alert by using the tools He has provided for us.

"Do not touch my anointed ones."

PSALM 105:15 NASB

That First Cup

Many people wouldn't dream of starting their day without a cup of coffee. They count on that "first cup of the day" to wake them up and get them going. Others have discovered an even more potent day- starter: first-thing-in-the-morning prayer.

For some, this is a prayer voiced to God before getting out of bed. For others, it is a planned time of prayer between getting dressed and leaving for work. For still others, it is a commitment to get to work half an hour early to spend quiet, focused time in prayer before the workday begins.

Henry Ward Beecher, one of the most notable preachers of the last century, had this to say about starting the day with prayer:

> *In the morning, prayer is the key that opens to us the treasure of God's mercies and blessings. The first act of the soul in early morning should be a draught at the heavenly fountain. It will sweeten the taste for the day.*
>
> *. . . And if you tarry long so sweetly at the throne, you will come out of the closet as the high priest of Israel came from the awful ministry at the altar of incense, suffused all over with the heavenly fragrance of that communion.*[45]

A popular song in Christian groups several years ago said, "Fill my cup, Lord; I lift it up, Lord. Come and quench this thirsting of my soul. Bread of heaven, feed me till I want no more; Fill my cup, fill it up and make me whole."[46]

    Morning prayer fills your cup to overflowing with peace. Then, as you have contact with other people at home and at work, you can pour that same peace into them. And the good news is—unlimited free refills are readily available any time your cup becomes empty throughout the day!

In the morning my prayer comes
before you.

PSALM 88:13 NKJV

Journey Toward Sunrise

When Moses led the children of Israel out of Egypt, the people immediately experienced great joy for deliverance from bondage. However, as they traveled through the wilderness toward the Promised Land, fear of the unknown would often take hold of their hearts. The following excerpt by Louise Haskins, taken from *Traveling Toward Sunrise*, captures the essence of how all of us press on into unknown territory by simply trusting God:

> *These travelers were time's valiant great hearts. They were journeying on the star road making their way through an inspiring land, a desert waste upheld by hope of a glorious new day, a tomorrow morning, when night with its darkness and shadows would be left far behind.*
>
> *Travelers whose hopes were fixed on what was before and beyond; men of faith who followed the gleam loyally, right through to the very end; road-makers, presenting an unparalleled example of courage and bravery; men of vision, always looking ahead, never behind.*
>
> *What an inspiring, challenging thought as we . . . begin our journey, traveling toward sunrise. Let us begin by filling the air with songs of rejoicing, with songs not sighs, for we are wayfarers of the infinite, traveling to the land where dawns are begotten and glory has its dwelling place, where life begins, not ends, and where there is eternal springtime.*

And I said to the man who stood at the gate of the year,
"Give me light that I may tread safely into the unknown!"
And he replied: "Go out into the darkness and put your
hand into the Hand of God; That shall be to you better than
light and safer than a known way." So I went forth, and
finding the Hand of God, trod gladly into the night.
And He led me toward the hills and the breaking of
the day in the lone East.[47]

As you read this, you may be facing tremendous opportunities or overwhelming difficulties. In either case, put
your hand into God's hand and walk with Him. Let Him
give you comfort and wisdom as you move toward your
promised land.

The children of Israel . . .
journeyed from . . . the wilderness
. . . toward the sunrising.

NUMBERS 21:10-11
KJV

Everyday Talk

The banquet hall is festively adorned with beautiful flowers and ribbons. Across the front of the room a large banner reads, "A Golden Congratulations for a Golden Couple." It is their fiftieth wedding anniversary, and family and friends have gathered from far and near to pay tribute to them. The four children each take a turn at describing their fondest memories and greatest lessons learned from their parents. Then the cake is cut, pictures are taken, and everyone enjoys visiting with one another.

Too soon, the afternoon concludes. Friends say good-bye; family members repack mementos in the cars and everyone leaves. Later that evening, one of the grandchildren asks, "What is the secret, Grandma, to being happily married for fifty years?"

Without hesitation, her grandmother replies, "We were always able to talk about everything."

Recent research supports her conclusion. A study of couples happily married for more than twenty-five years found only one thing they all had in common—each couple "chitchatted" with each other daily. Perhaps, since they already know how to converse with one another, they are more able to talk out their differences when tough times come. The same most likely holds true for our relationship with God. If we commune with Him regularly, then we will automatically turn to Him first when crisis comes.

Have you had a quiet time talking with God today?

Let your conversation be always full of grace.

COLOSSIANS 4:6

Without Words

As with many memorials, the Franklin Delano Roosevelt memorial in Washington, D.C., was built after years of debate. Women's groups demanded that Eleanor be given appropriate recognition. Activists for the disabled ardently believed that FDR should be portrayed in his wheelchair. On and on, the debates raged. Finally, in spite of all the controversy, it was completed.

The memorial gives testimony to the fact that President Roosevelt and his wife Eleanor served America during some of its darkest years. It is a fitting design because as visitors approach it, nothing really stands out. All one sees is a flat granite wall, perhaps twenty feet in height, with a simple quote from FDR; but this is just the beginning.

The memorial stretches directly away from the entrance. After rounding the wall, visitors move from area to area; every one marked by unique stillness. Each succeeding area is creatively set apart from the previous one making it a tribute in its own right. Visitors find themselves looking at human-sized sculptures of men and women standing in breadlines, reading quotes decrying the savagery of war, staring eye to eye with Eleanor Roosevelt and eventually looking up and across to see FDR in his wheelchair with his Scottish terrier beside him.

The strength of the memorial comes from its ability to draw the visitor into the presence of one man's passionate belief in serving his country. The impact of the memorial is to make each visitor more aware of the awesome responsibility of leadership—not just the leadership of presidents, but leadership of all people.

Whenever you have doubts about your purpose, remember the words of Martin Luther King, Jr., "Everyone can be great because everyone can serve."

Show proper respect to everyone.

I PETER 2:17

Feel the Power!

Pope John XXIII was quoted as saying, "It often happens that I wake at night and begin to think about a serious problem and decide I must tell the Pope about it. Then I wake up completely and remember that I am the Pope."

How often we imagine that the solution to our problems, the cure for our ailments, or the guarantee for our happiness lies with someone or something outside ourselves. But do we really have so little power?

Martha Washington thought otherwise, stating, "I have learned from experience that the greater part of our happiness or misery depends on our dispositions and not on our circumstances. We carry the seeds with us in our minds wherever we go.

Just think about it. How dramatically your life could change if you knew you had the seeds to your happiness waiting inside, longing to blossom whenever you would allow it? From Mother Teresa, in her book, *A Gift to God*, we can learn how to let those seeds spring to life.

We all long for Heaven where God is but we have it in our power to be in Heaven with Him right now—to be happy with Him at this very moment. But being happy with Him now means:

- *loving as He loves,*
- *helping as He helps,*
- *giving as He gives,*
- *serving as He serves,*
- *rescuing as He rescues,*
- *being with Him for all the twenty-four hours,*
- *touching Him in His distressing disguise.*

The fruit of the Spirit is love, joy, peace, patience, kindness, goodness, faithfulness, gentleness, self-control.

GALATIANS 5:22-23
NASB

Like a Newborn Babe

I n 1994, Jim Gleason underwent a life-saving heart transplant at age 51. After one of the most extreme surgeries imaginable, many asked how it felt to live with a new heart. His analogy was "... like being born again, but with 50 years of memories and experiences built in ..."

He tells of coming home just ten days after his transplant. He wanted to go for a short walk around the yard. Accompanied by his daughter, he gazed in wonder at the green grass after weeks of hospital-room walls.

> *I stopped walking. "Look at that!" I exclaimed to Mary. I was pointing to our small maple tree, so vibrant with the colors of that crisp, clear fall day. Then I spied a grasshopper and, like the young child, exclaimed in glee, "Look at that! A grasshopper!"*
>
> *Her response, in disbelief at try reaction, was an almost sarcastic, "Well, if that's exciting, look here—a lady bug!"*

After many years with his new heart, Jim still cherishes life's simple pleasures. And when is the danger of losing that gift greatest? "As friends and family wish you would return to being 'normal,'" he reflects. "I struggle to never become 'normal' in that sense again."[48]

With God's help, we too can walk in newness of life—no surgery required. Give thanks that we don't have to be "normal."

"I will give you a new
heart and put a new spirit
within you;
I will take the heart of
stone out of your flesh
and give you a heart of
flesh."

EZEKIEL 36:26 NKJV

Walls

The following lines from poet Robert Frost's famous work "Mending Walls" hit right at the heart of the challenge of maintaining proper relationships:

I let my neighbor know beyond the hill;
And on a day we meet to walk the line
And set the wall between us once again.[49]

The poem both celebrates tradition and pokes fun at it at the same time. Many individuals, over the years, have debated its most famous line: "Good fences make good neighbors."

Frost himself takes issue with the need for carefully maintained boundaries when he attempts to get a rise out of his neighbor by asking, "Why do they make good neighbors?"

Receiving no response, he goes on to say, "Something there is that doesn't love a wall, that wants it down." Still no response, and in the closing lines he likens his neighbor to "an old stone savage armed, who will not go behind his father's saying."

Why do we seem to build walls between others and ourselves or between God and ourselves? Is it perhaps because we fear we may become vulnerable to rejection? Or do we simply feel an irresistible need to stake our claim to what we want as our own? In either case, it takes much courage to maintain proper respect for one another without building walls that separate us inappropriately.

Robert Frost urges us to be careful to know what we might be "walling in or out and to whom we might give offense" upon building walls. Walls are serious business and we need to be careful how we use them. Erected incorrectly, they create inequality and hatred. Erected right, they can make for good relationships.

The wall of Jerusalem also is broken down.

NEHEMIAH 1:3 KJV

Proper Form

A father spent the afternoon with his three-year-old daughter. An avid golfer, he practiced with his clubs in the yard while she played nearby. As he prepared for each swing, he would look to his left to aim the shot, then back to his right to make sure the child was out of harm's way—only then would he take his shot.

Soon, he noticed that his daughter was also playing golf. She had taken a stick to use as a club, and he watched as she set her "club," carefully looked left, then right, then took her shot. In her perception, proper golfing form required that you look both ways before you swing.

Whether we realize it or not, our example leaves an impression on others. In the 1800s, English minister Charles Spurgeon put it this way:

> *A man's life is always more forcible than his speech. When men take stock of him they reckon his deeds as dollars and his words as pennies. If his life and doctrine disagree the mass of onlookers accept his practice and reject his preaching.*

When Jesus said, "You are the light of the world," He wasn't speaking only of our verbal witness. The most profound message we will ever send is the one we live on a day-to-day basis. It's never more important than when we don't know anyone is paying attention because Someone is always paying attention.

Like as he who called you
is holy, be ye yourselves
also holy in all manner of
living; because it is written,
Ye shall be holy;
for I am holy.

1 PETER 1:15-16 ASV

Grace Tickets

A Bible teacher taught about God's "Grace Tickets." She said God makes Himself available to us no matter how many times we reach out for an extra Grace Ticket. His grace is available to us in liberal amounts. She even prayed that she would have the wisdom to know when to reach out and take another.

When the alarm goes off at 5:30am, it is all too easy to slip a hand from under the covers and push that snooze button to allow for ten more minutes of sleep. You might repeat the same involuntary movement every ten minutes until 6am when the clock radio is programmed to come on.

The minute the announcer s voice is heard, you are immediately jolted from bed realizing you have overslept and must do in twenty minutes what would normally take fifty. The antics that take place in that room are worthy of a feature on a television comedy show.

We all need several of God's Grace Tickets for times in our lives when we attempt to put God and His timing on hold. Yet God has made Himself available to us every minute of the day. We are privileged to call out to Him no matter how severe or minuscule our situation. His grace is sufficient for each of us—at all times. He never runs out. It is up to us to open our eyes each morning and reach out to the Giver of all Grace Tickets.

Many of us are in the habit of pushing the "snooze button" on God's time. However, He is patiently waiting with a whole stack of Grace Tickets for us. Why not set your clock by His?

"The one who comes to me I will certainly not cast out."

JOHN 6:37 NASB

Good Morning, Lord

There is something extraordinarily special about early morning devotions. Before the hectic day begins with its noise and numerous distractions, there is usually a calm that is uncommon to any other time of the day, a peaceful prerequisite for entering into the prayer closet with Christ. Christ set an example for us when He rose up early and prayed.

Morning is the first step to the list of "things to do" written out the night before and a world of unknown plans prepared by God for us to become acquainted with. Morning is a wonderfully private time where intimate conversation and gentle responses can take place between God and His children. This is a time to listen to the very heart of God.

Oswald Chambers said, "Get an inner chamber in which to pray where no one knows you are praying, shut the door, and talk to God in secret. Have no other motive than to know your Father in heaven. It is impossible to conduct your life as a disciple without definite times of secret prayer."

Between Midnight and Morning
You that have faith to look with fearless eyes
Beyond the tragedy of a world of strife,
And trust that out of night and death shall rise
The dawn of ampler life;
Rejoice, whatever anguish rend your heart,

GOOD MORNING, GOD

That God has given you, for a priceless dower,
To live in these great times and have your part
In Freedom's crowning hour;
That we may tell jour sons who see the light
High in heaven—their heritage to take—
"I saw the powers of darkness put to flight!
I saw the morning break!"

Owen Seaman

In the morning, O Lord, thou wilt
hear my voice; in the morning I
will order my prayer to thee and
eagerly watch.

PSALM 5:3 NASB

References

Endnotes

[1] "Morning Has Broken." Eleanor Farjeon. The *United Methodist Hymnal* (Nashville. TN: The United Methodist Publishing House. 1989). p. 145.

[2] Barbara J. Winter

[3] *The Joy of Working.* Denis Waitley and Reni Witt (New York, NY: Dodd Mead and Company. 1985). P. 253.

[4] "The Endless Streetcar Ride into the Night, and the Tinfoil Noose," Jean Shepherd, in *The Riverside Reader*, Vol. 5. (Boston, MA: Houghton Mifflin Company. 1985). p. 17.

[5] *Knight's Master Book of 4,000 Illustrations.* Walter B. Knight (Grand Rapids, MI: William B. Eerdmans Publishing Co.. 1956). P. 93.

[6] *Reader's Digest.* September 1991, pp. 115-116.

[7] Joseph Addison.

[8] *Reader's Digest.* January 1999, pp. 58-61.

[9] "Putting Away Childish Things." David Seamands, *The Inspirational Study Bible.* Max Lucado. gen. ed. (Dallas: Word Publishing, 1995) pp. 35-36

[10] *Merriam-Webster's Collegiate Dictionary Tenth Edition,* copyright © 2001 by Merriam-Webster, Incorporated.

[11] *Reader's Digest.* December 1992, pp. 101-104.

[12] *Reader's Digest.* December 1991, pp. 96-100.

[13] *The Finishing Touch.* Charles R. Swindoll (Dallas: Word Publishing, 1994). pp. 186-187.

[14] *The Methodist Reporter.* November/December 1995, editorial section.

[15] Gary Johnson. *Reader's Digest.* September 1991, pp. 164-165.

[16] "Churchill, Sir Winston Leonard Spencer," *Microsoft® Encarta® 98 Encyclopedia.* ©1993-1997 Microsoft Corporation. All rights reserved.

[17]Ibid.

[18]*Illustrations Unlimited.* James Hewitt, ed. (Wheaton: Tyndale House, 1988), p. 159.

[19]*Who Said That?* George Sweeting (Chicago, IL: Moody Press. 1995.

[20]"The Endless Streetcar Ride into the Night, and the Tinfoil Noose." Jean Shepherd, in *The Riverside Reader.* Vol. 1 (Boston, MA: Houghton Mifflin Company, 1985), p. 32.

[21]Ibid, p. 37.

[22]Ibid.

[23]*A Guide to Prayer.* Reuben P. Job and Norman Shawchuck (Nashville: The Upper Room. 1983), p. 176.

[24]*Pacific Discover.* Spring 1994, p. 20.

[25]Swindoll. *Hand Me Another Brick* (Nashville: Thomas Nelson. 1978). pp. 82, 88.

[26]*White Fang.* Jack London (New York. NY: Tom Doherty Associates. Inc., 1988).

[27]Ibid.

[28]*Spiritual Disciplines for the Christian Life*, Donald S. Whitney (Colorado Springs: NavPress. 1991), p. 37.

[29]From "Words of Love by Mother Teresa" in *Education for Democracy.* Benjamin R. Barber and Richard M. Battistoni, eds., (Dubuque: Kendall/Hunt Publishing Company, 1993).

[30]Ibid.

[31]*San Luis Obispo Telegraph-Tribune* January 31, 1996, B-3.

[32]Quote from Ghandi, *A Guide to Prayer*, Reuben P. Job and Norman Shawchuck (Nashville: The Upper Room. 1983), p. 234.

[33]*Today in the Word*, Moody Bible Institute. January 1992, p. 8.

[34]*Legacy of a Pack Rat.* Ruth Bell Graham (Nashville: Thomas Nelson, 1989), p. 49.

[35]Judy Seymour. "The Freeway Not Taken: Lake Route Worth the Slower Pace." *Minneapolis Star Tribune*, May 12, 1997, p. 15A.

[36]*Daily Bread*, July 20, 1992.

[37]Author Unknown.

[38]Kovachevich Radomir.

[39] *Today in the Word.* February 1991, p. 10.

[40]*Book of Prayers,* Robert Van de Weyer. ed. (New York, NY: Harper Collins. 1993), p. 67.

[41] *Christianity Today.* December 9, 1996. Vol. 40, No. 14, p. 80.

[42] *Today in the Word.* September 2, 1992.

[43]Maya Angelou. *Wouldn't Take Nothin' for My Journey Now,* (New York, NY: Random House, 1993), p. 62.

[44] *The Harper Collins Book of Prayers,* Robert Van de Weyer, ed. (New York, NY: Harper Collins. 1993), pp. 389-390.

[45] *The New Dictionary of Thoughts,* Tyron Edwards, ed. (New York, NY: Standard Book Company, 1963), p. 506.

[46]"Fill My Cup, Lord," Richard Blanchard. *Chorus Book* (Dallas, TX: Word, Inc., 1971).

[47]"Introduction." Louise Haskins, *Traveling Toward Sunrise.* Mrs. Charles Cowman, ed. (Grand Rapids, MI: Zondervan Publishing House, no pub. date), p. 1.

[48]Jim Gleason (Transplant Recipient Support List: trnsplnt@wuvmd.wustl.edu).

[49]"Mending Walls." Robert Frost, in *Writing for Change: A Community Reader* (San Francisco, CA: McGraw-Hill. Inc., 1995), pp. 123-124.